Machine Learning with SAS®

Special Collection

Foreword by
Saratendu Sethi

sas.com/books

Table of Contents

Free SAS® e-Books:
Special Collection

In this series, we have carefully curated a collection of papers that introduces and provides context to the various areas of analytics. Topics covered illustrate the power of SAS solutions that are available as tools for data analysis, highlighting a variety of commonly used techniques.

Discover more free SAS e-books!
support.sas.com/freesasebooks

 sas.com/books
for additional books and resources.

About This Book

What Does This Collection Cover?

Machine learning is a branch of artificial intelligence (AI) that develops algorithms that allow computers to learn from examples without being explicitly programmed. Machine learning identifies patterns in the data and models the results. These descriptive models enable a better understanding of the underlying insights the data offers. Machine learning is a powerful tool with many applications, from real-time fraud detection, the Internet of Things (IoT), recommender systems, and smart cars. It will not be long before some form of machine learning is integrated into all machines, augmenting the user experience and automatically running many processes intelligently.

SAS offers many different solutions to use machine learning to model and predict your data. The papers included in this special collection demonstrate how cutting-edge machine learning techniques can benefit your data analysis.

The following papers are excerpts from the SAS Global Users Group *Proceedings*. For more SUGI and SAS Global Forum *Proceedings*, visit the online versions of the Proceedings.

More helpful resources are available at support.sas.com and sas.com/books.

We Want to Hear from You

SAS Press books are written *by* SAS users *for* SAS users. We welcome your participation in their development and your feedback on SAS Press books that you are using. Please visit sas.com/books to

- Sign up to review a book
- Request information on how to become a SAS Press author
- Recommend a topic
- Provide feedback on a book

Do you have questions about a SAS Press book that you are reading? Contact the author through saspress@sas.com.

Foreword

The term *machine learning* was coined by Arthur Lee Samuel to represent a class of self-learning programs he created to play the game of checkers. It is a data-driven system focused on selecting the best approach for a specific analytic problem, such as regression, classification, or pattern recognition. Machine learning algorithms identify patterns in data to provide descriptive models of the data. A key driver for machine learning is how well the derived model can be generalized to new data, thus leading to better business decisions and the ability to predict outcomes in the digital world.

For more than four decades, SAS has been recognized for its innovation and application of machine learning to help companies tackle the toughest business problems, ranging from real-time fraud detection, the Internet of Things (IoT), recommender systems, and smart cars. Using state-of-the-art techniques, such as deep learning and kernel approximation, SAS allows you to build machine learning models and implement iterative machine learning processes. With the drive toward artificial intelligence (AI) and automation, it will not be long before some form of machine learning is integrated into every aspects of our lives, augmenting the user experience and automatically running many processes intelligently.

SAS offers many different solutions to use machine learning to model and predict your data, and several groundbreaking papers have been written to demonstrate how to use these techniques. We have carefully selected a handful of these from recent SAS Global Forum papers to introduce you to the topics and to let you sample what each has to offer.

An Overview of SAS® Visual Data Mining and Machine Learning on SAS® Viya®

Jonathan Wexler, Susan Haller, and Radhikha Myneni, SAS Institute Inc.

Solving modern business problems often requires analytics that encompass multiple algorithmic disciplines, data that is both structured and unstructured, multiple programming languages, and – most importantly – collaboration within and across teams of varying skill sets. SAS® Visual Data Mining and Machine Learning on SAS® Viya® surfaces in-memory machine-learning techniques such as gradient boosting, factorization machines, neural networks, and much more through its interactive visual interface, SAS® Studio tasks, procedures, and a Python client. This paper shows you how to solve business problems, quickly and collaboratively, using SAS Visual Data Mining and Machine Learning on SAS Viya.

Interactive Modeling in SAS® Visual Analytics

Don Chapman, SAS Institute Inc.

This paper illustrates how the use of the highly interactive, visual SAS® Visual Data Mining and Machine Learning offering will not only make your data problems manageable but also engaging. This offering is composed of capabilities that range from data preparation to programmatic access to advanced machine learning in your language of choice. We focus on the case study of a day in the life of a data scientist who needs to solve a business problem quickly. How do they acquire the data and get it prepared for modeling? How do they explore the data to understand its characteristics? How do they generate and compare models? How do they document those insights and apply them to solving a business problem?

Open Your Mind: Use Cases for SAS® and Open-Source Analytics

Tuba Islam, SAS Institute Inc.

Data scientists need analytical tools and algorithms, whether commercial or open source, and will always have some favorites. But how do you decide when to use what? And how can you integrate their use to your maximum advantage? This paper some examples to show the deployment of both SAS® and open-source analytical tools to increase productivity and efficiency in your enterprise ecosystem. We look at an analytical business flow for marketing using SAS and R algorithms in SAS® Enterprise Miner™ for developing a predictive model, and then operationalizing and automating that model for scoring, performance monitoring and retraining. There are also suggestions for using Python and SAS integration in a Jupyter Notebook environment.

Automated Hyperparameter Tuning for Effective Machine Learning

Patrick Koch, Brett Wujek, Oleg Golovidov, and Steven Gardner, SAS Institute Inc.

Machine learning is a form of self-calibration of predictive models that are built from training data. Machine learning predictive modeling algorithms are commonly used to find hidden value in big data. Machine learning predictive modeling algorithms are governed by "hyperparameters" that have no clear defaults agreeable to a wide range of applications. This paper presents an automatic tuning implementation that uses local search optimization for tuning hyperparameters of modeling algorithms in SAS® Visual Data Mining and Machine Learning. Given the inherent expense of training numerous candidate models, the paper addresses efficient distributed and parallel paradigms for training and tuning models on the SAS® Viya® platform. It also presents sample tuning results that demonstrate improved model accuracy and offers recommendations for efficient and effective model tuning.

Random Forests with Approximate Bayesian Model Averaging

Tiny du Toit, North-West University, South Africa; André de Waal, SAS Institute Inc.

Random forests occupies a leading position amongst ensemble models and have shown to be very successful in data mining and analytics competitions. A random forest is an ensemble of decision trees that often produce more accurate results than a single decision tree. The predictions of the individual trees in the forest are averaged to produce a final prediction. The question now arises whether a better or more accurate final prediction cannot be obtained by a more intelligent use of the trees in the forest. In this paper two novel approaches to solving this problem are presented and the results compared to that obtained with the standard random forest approach.

Methods of Multinomial Classification Using Support Vector Machines

Ralph Abbey, Taiping He, and Tao Wang, SAS Institute Inc.

The support vector machine (SVM) algorithm is a popular binary classification technique used in the fields of machine learning, data mining, and predictive analytics. Since the introduction of the SVM algorithm in 1995 (Cortes and Vapnik 1995), researchers and practitioners in these fields have shown significant interest in using and improving SVMs. Two established methods of using SVMs in multinomial classification are the one-versus-all approach and the one-versus-one approach. This paper describes how to use SAS® software to implement these two methods of multinomial classification, with emphasis on both training the model and scoring new data. A variety of data sets are used to illustrate the pros and cons of each method.

Factorization Machines: A New Tool for Sparse Data

Jorge Silva and Raymond E. Wright, SAS Institute Inc.

Factorization models, which include factorization machines as a special case, are a broad class of models popular in statistics and machine learning. Factorization machines are well suited to very high-cardinality, sparsely observed transactional data. This paper presents the new FACTMAC procedure, which implements factorization machines in SAS® Visual Data Mining and Machine Learning. Thanks to a highly parallel stochastic gradient descent optimization solver, PROC FACTMAC can quickly handle data sets that contain tens of millions of rows.

Building Bayesian Network Classifiers Using the HPBNET Procedure

Ye Liu, Weihua Shi, and Wendy Czika, SAS Institute Inc.

A Bayesian network is a directed acyclic graphical model that represents probability relationships and conditional independence structure between random variables. SAS® Enterprise Miner™ implements a Bayesian network primarily as a classification tool; it supports naïve Bayes, tree-augmented naïve Bayes, Bayesian-network-augmented naïve Bayes, parent-child Bayesian network, and Markov blanket Bayesian network classifiers. This paper compares the performance of Bayesian network classifiers to other popular classification methods such as classification tree, neural network, logistic regression, and support vector machines.

Stacked Ensemble Models for Improved Prediction Accuracy

Funda Güneş, Russ Wolfinger, and Pei-Yi Tan, SAS Institute Inc.

Ensemble modeling is now a well-established means for improving prediction accuracy; it enables you to average out noise from diverse models and thereby enhance the generalizable signal. Basic stacked ensemble techniques combine predictions from multiple machine learning algorithms and use these predictions as inputs to second-level learning models. This paper shows how you can generate a diverse set of models by various methods such as forest, gradient boosted decision trees, factorization machines, and logistic regression and then combine them with stacked-ensemble techniques such as hill climbing, gradient boosting, and nonnegative least squares in SAS® Visual Data Mining and Machine Learning.

We hope these selections give you a useful overview of the many tools and techniques that are available to incorporate cutting-edge machine learning techniques into your data analysis.

Saratendu Sethi, SAS Institute Inc.
Head, Artificial Intelligence and Machine Learning R&D

Saratendu Sethi is Head of Artificial Intelligence and Machine Learning R&D at SAS Institute. He leads SAS' software development and research teams for Artificial Intelligence, Machine Learning, Cognitive Computing, Deep Learning, and Text Analytics. Saratendu has extensive experience in building global R&D teams, launching new products and business strategies. Perennially fascinated by how technology enables a creative life, he is a staunch believer in transforming powerful algorithms into innovative technologies. At SAS, his teams develop machine learning, cognitive- and semantic-enriched capabilities for unstructured data and multimedia analytics. He joined SAS Institute through the acquisition of Teragram Corporation, where he was responsible for the development of natural language processing and text analytics technologies. Before joining Teragram, Saratendu held research positions at the IBM Almaden Research Center and at Boston University, specializing in computer vision, pattern recognition, and content-based search.

Paper SAS1492-2017

An Overview of SAS® Visual Data Mining and Machine Learning on SAS® Viya

Jonathan Wexler, Susan Haller, and Radhikha Myneni, SAS Institute Inc., Cary, NC

ABSTRACT

Machine learning is in high demand. Whether you are a citizen data scientist who wants to work interactively or you are a hands-on data scientist who wants to code, you have access to the latest analytic techniques with SAS® Visual Data Mining and Machine Learning on SAS® Viya. This offering surfaces in-memory machine-learning techniques such as gradient boosting, factorization machines, neural networks, and much more through its interactive visual interface, SAS® Studio tasks, procedures, and a Python client. Learn about this multi-faceted new product and see it in action.

INTRODUCTION

Solving modern business problems often requires analytics that encompass multiple algorithmic disciplines, data that is both structured and unstructured, multiple programming languages, and – most importantly – collaboration within and across teams of varying skill sets. Addressing and solving business problems should not be constrained by technology. Technology enables analysts to solve problems from multiple angles. Likewise, computing power is cheap. Problems that were once deemed unsolvable using neural networks can now be run in mere seconds.

This paper shows you how to solve business problems, quickly and collaboratively, using SAS Visual Data Mining and Machine Learning on SAS Viya. This new offering enables you to interactively explore your data to uncover 'signal' in your data. Next you can programmatically analyze your data using a rich set of SAS procedures covering Statistics, Machine Learning, and Text Mining. You can add new input features using in-memory SAS DATA step. Utilize new tasks in SAS Studio on the SAS Viya platform to automatically generate the SAS code. If you prefer to write Python, access SAS Viya methods with the Python API. No matter the interface or language, SAS Viya enables you to start your analysis and continue forward without any roadblocks.

In this paper, you will learn how to access these methods through a case study.

SAS VISUAL DATA MINING AND MACHINE LEARNING ON SAS VIYA

SAS Viya is the foundation upon which the analytical toolset in this paper is installed. The components are modular by design. At its core, SAS Viya is built upon a common analytic framework, using 'actions'. These actions are atomic analytic activities, such as selecting variables, building models, generating results, and outputting score code. As shown in Figure 1, these actions can be accessed via SAS procedures, SAS applications, RESTful services, Java, Lua, and Python.

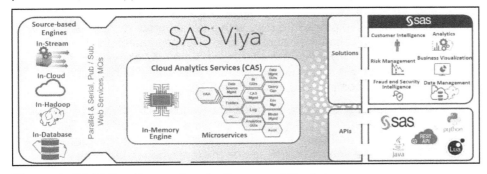

Figure 1. SAS Viya Ecosystem Is Open and Modular

SUPPORTED SAS VIYA ALGORITHMS

From a data mining and machine learning perspective, SAS Visual Data Mining and Machine Learning on SAS Viya enables end-to-end analytics - data wrangling, model building, and model assessment.

As shown in Table 1, the following methods are available to users:

Data Wrangling	Modeling
Binning	Logistic Regression
Cardinality	Linear Regression
Imputation	Generalized Linear Models
Transformations	Nonlinear Regression
Transpose	Ordinary Least Squares Regression
SQL	Partial Least Squares Regression
Sampling	Quantile Regression
Variable Selection	Decision Trees
Principal Components Analysis (PCA)	Forest
K-Means Clustering	Gradient Boosting
Moving Window PCA	Neural Network
Robust PCA	Support Vector Machines
	Factorization Machines
	Network / Community Detection
	Text Mining
	Support Vector Data Description

Table 1. Analytic Methods Available in SAS Visual Data Mining and Machine Learning on SAS Viya

You will experience increased productivity when using the aforementioned methods. All of these methods run in-memory, and take advantage of the parallel processing ability of your underlying infrastructure. The more nodes you have; the higher degree of parallelism you will experience when running. Once data is loaded to memory up-front, you can run sequential procedures against the same table in memory, eliminating the need to drop the data to disk after each run. You can continue your analysis using the same data in-memory. If the memory of your problem requires more memory than is available, the processing will continue over to disk.

There were numerous analytic innovations that we introduced with SAS Viya. At the head of the class is hyperparameter autotuning (Koch, Wujek, Golovidov, and Gardner 2017). When data scientists tune models, they train the models to determine the best model parameters to relate the input to a target. When they tune a model, they determine the architecture or best algorithmic hyperparameters that maximize predictability on an independent data set. Autotuning eliminates the need for random grid search or in a SAS user's case, running repetitive procedure calls with different properties. As shown in Figure 2, Autotuning uses a local search optimization methodology to intelligently search the hyperparameter space for the best combination of values that addresses the model objective – that is, misclassification, Lift, KS, and so on. Autotuning is available for Decision Trees, Neural Networks, Support Vector Machines, Forests, Gradient Boosting, and Factorization Machines.

Also new in SAS Viya are enhanced feature engineering techniques like Robust PCA (RPCA), Moving Window PCA, and the capability to detect outliers using Support Vector Data Description (SVDD). Robust PCA decomposes an input matrix into low-rank and sparse matrices. The low-rank matrix is more stable as the distortions in the data are moved into the sparse matrix, hence the term robust. Moving Window PCA captures the changes in principal components over time using sliding windows and you can choose RPCA to be performed in each window. SVDD is a machine learning technique where the model builds a minimum radius sphere around the training data and scores new observations by comparing the observation's distance from sphere center with the sphere radius. Thus, an observation outside the sphere is classified as an outlier.

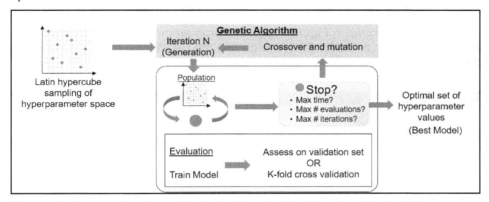

Figure 2. Autotuning Uses Optimization to Find the Best Set of Hyperparameters to Minimize Error

SAS VISUAL DATA MINING AND MACHINE LEARNING PRIMARY ANALYTIC INTERFACES

There are three primary interfaces we will cover in this paper. From within each tool, you can extend your analysis into one of the others. Data can be shared, and models can be extended and compared.

VISUAL ANALYTICS

SAS Visual Analytics enables drag-and-drop, exploratory visualization and modeling. Data must be loaded into memory, otherwise known as SAS Cloud Analytic Services (CAS). Once in CAS, you can interactively explore your data using visuals such as scatter plots, waterfall charts, bubble plots, time series plots and many more. As shown in Figure 3, you can further analyze your data using a set of statistics techniques including Clustering, Decision Trees, Generalized Linear Models, Linear Regression, and Logistic Regression. You can expand upon these models using the latest machine learning techniques including Factorization Machines, Forests, Gradient Boosting, Neural Networks, and Support Vector Machines.

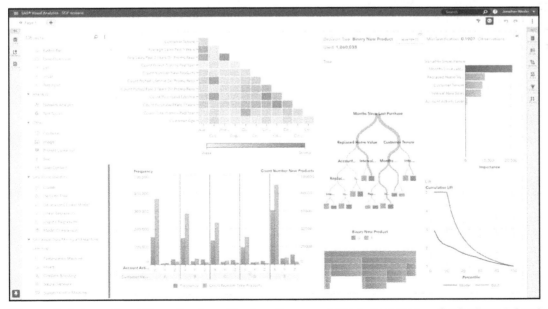

Figure 3. Interactive Visualization, Exploration, and Modeling Using SAS Visual Analytics

SAS STUDIO

SAS® Studio enables browser-based, programmatic access to the methods in SAS Viya. Using a modern, easy-to-use interface, you can run the exact same methods, and get the exact same answers as you would have with SAS Visual Analytics. As shown in Figure 4, you can programmatically run the methods from SAS Viya using in-memory procedures and SAS DATA step. Yes, the SAS DATA step now runs in-memory! There are several SAS Studio tasks that serve as code generators, so you have a way to learn and run these methods.

Figure 4. Access the SAS Viya Methods Using the SAS Language within SAS Studio

JUPYTER NOTEBOOK / PYTHON API

You can access the SAS Viya methods using the Python API to SAS Viya. The same methods that you can access in SAS Visual Analytics and SAS Studio are exposed from Python. A shown in Figure 5, you can access SAS Viya using a Jupyter notebook. Using a familiar Python construct, you can programmatically analyze your data, without any prior SAS knowledge.

4

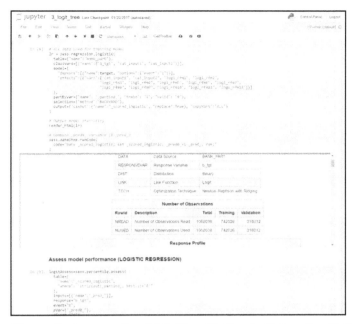

Figure 5. Access the SAS Viya Methods Using the Python API to SAS Viya

CASE STUDY

The BANK data set contains more than one million observations (rows) and 24 variables (columns) for this case study. The data set comes from a large financial services firm and represents consumers' home equity lines of credit, their automobile loans, and other types of short to medium-term credit instruments. Note that the data has been anonymized and transformed to conform to the regulation guidelines.

Though three target variables are available in the data set, the primary focus is on the binary target variable B_TGT, which indicates consumer accounts that bought at least one product in the previous campaign season. A campaign season at the bank runs for half a year and encompasses all marketing efforts to motivate the purchase (contracting) of the bank's financial services products. Campaign promotions are categorized into direct and indirect -- direct promotions consist of sales offers to a particular account that involve an incentive while indirect promotions are marketing efforts that do not involve an incentive.

In addition to the account identifier (**Account ID**), the following tables describe the variables in the data set:

Name	Label	Description
B_TGT	Tgt Binary New Product	A binary target variable. Accounts coded with a 1 contracted for at least one product in the previous campaign season. Accounts coded with a 0 did not contract for a product in the previous campaign season.
INT_TGT	Tgt Interval New Sales	The amount of financial services product (sum of sales) per account in the previous campaign season, denominated in US dollars.
CNT_TGT	Tgt Count Number New Products	The number of financial services products (count) per account in the previous campaign season.

Table 2. Target Variables Quantify Account Responses over the Current Campaign Season.

Name	Label	Description
CAT_INPUT1	Category 1 Account Activity Level	A three-level categorical variable that codes the activity of each account. • X → high activity. The account enters the current campaign period with a lot of products. • Y → average activity. • Z → low activity.
CAT_INPUT2	Category 2 Customer Value Level	A five-level (A-E) categorical variable that codes customer value. For example, the most profitable and creditworthy customers are coded with an A.

Table 3. Categorical Inputs Summarize Account-level Attributes Related to the Propensity to Buy Products and Other Characteristics Related to Profitability and Creditworthiness. These Variables Have Been Transformed to Anonymize Account-level Information and to Mitigate Quality Issues Related to Excessive Cardinality.

Name	Label	Description
RFM1	RFM1 Average Sales Past 3 Years	Average sales amount attributed to each account over the past three years
RFM2	RFM2 Average Sales Lifetime	Average sales amount attributed to each account over the account's tenure
RFM3	RFM3 Avg Sales Past 3 Years Dir Promo Resp	Average sales amount attributed to each account in the past three years in response to a direct promotion
RFM4	RFM4 Last Product Purchase Amount	Amount of the last product purchased
RFM5	RFM5 Count Purchased Past 3 Years	Number of products purchased in the past three years
RFM6	RFM6 Count Purchased Lifetime	Total number of products purchased in each account's tenure.
RFM7	RFM7 Count Prchsd Past 3 Years Dir Promo Resp	Number of products purchased in the previous three years in response to a direct promotion
RFM8	RFM8 Count Prchsd Lifetime Dir Promo Resp	Total number of products purchased in the account's tenure in response to a direct promotion
RFM9	RFM9 Months Since Last Purchase	Months since the last product purchase
RFM10	RFM10 Count Total Promos Past Year	Number of total promotions received by each account in the past year
RFM11	RFM11 Count Direct Promos Past Year	Number of direct promotions received by each account in the past year
RFM12	RFM12 Customer Tenure	Customer tenure in months.

Table 4. Interval Inputs Provide Continuous Measures on Account-level Attributes Related to the

Recency, Frequency, and Sales Amounts (RFM). All Measures below Correspond to Activity Prior to the Current Campaign Season.

Name	Label	Description
DEMOG_AGE	Demog Customer Age	Average age in each account's demographic region
DEMOG_GENF	Demog Female Binary	A categorical variable that is 1 if the primary holder of the account if female and 0 otherwise.
DEMOG_GENM	Demog Male Binary	A categorical variable that is 1 if the primary holder of the account is male and 0 otherwise
DEMOG_HO	Demog Homeowner Binary	A categorical variable that is 1 if the primary holder of the account is a homeowner and 0 otherwise.
DEMOG_HOMEVAL	Demog Home Value	Average home value in each account's demographic region
DEMOG_INC	Demog Income	Average income in each account's demographic region
DEMOG_PR	Demog Percentage Retired	The percentage of retired people in each account's demographic region

Table 5. Demographic Variables Describe the Profile of Each Account in Terms of Income, Homeownership, and Other Characteristics.

LOAD LOCAL DATA TO IN-MEMORY LIBRARY

Before we start our analysis, we will use SAS Studio to load the local data to memory, so that it is accessible by our analytics team both visually and programmatically. We will then create a validation holdout set in order to assess our models.

The first LIBNAME statement automatically starts a CAS session, attached to the public caslib. Caslibs are in-memory locations that contain tables, access controls, and information about data sources. We are using the public caslib since this location is accessible by our team. In SAS Studio mycaslib is a library reference to the public caslib and will be referred to by SAS Viya procedures and any SAS DATA steps. The second LIBNAME statement is linked to the local file system that contains our SAS data set.

```
libname mycaslib cas caslib=public;
libname locallib 'your_local_library';
```

We will use PROC CASUTIL to load our local data to the public caslib. Using the 'promote' option enables us to make the data available to all CAS sessions. By default, tables in CAS sessions have local scope, so promoting enables you to access the in-memory table across multiple sessions and users.

```
proc casutil;
   load data=locallib.bank OUTCASLIB="public" casout="bank" promote;
run;
```

We will run PROC PARTITION to randomly separate our data into training and validation partitions. A new variable _partind_ will be assigned two numeric values: 1 for training data and 2 for validation data. The seed option allows you to re-create the random sample in future CAS sessions on the same CAS server. This is valuable when trying to reproduce results with multiple users. You should include the copyvars option if you want to keep all source variables in your partitioned data set.

```
proc partition data=mycaslib.bank partition samppct=70 seed=12345;
  by b_tgt;
  output out=mycaslib.bank_part copyvars=(_ALL_);
run;
```

BUILD MODELS INTERACTIVELY USING VISUAL ANALYTICS

Once the data is loaded and promoted to the public caslib, it is accessible from within SAS Visual Analytics. The first model we will create is a Gradient Boosting model, which trains a series of decision trees successively to fit the residual of the prediction from the earlier trees in the series. The target in this model is b_tgt. We will set the number of trees to 50. There are other regularization options such as Lasso and Ridge that can help prevent overfitting. As you change options, the visualization is recomputed in near real time, taking just a few seconds.

Note that misclassification for the validation partition is 0.1598. The first visualization, on the left, is the Variable Importance plot. This plot displays each variable's importance in the model. See that rfm5, rfm9, and demog_homeval are proportionately more important than the other predictors. The next plot is the Iteration plot, which indicates how well the model classified as the number of trees increased. In this case, the misclassification rate tails off after about 30 trees. The bottom right plot indicates how well the model assessed in terms of lift, misclassification, and ROC.

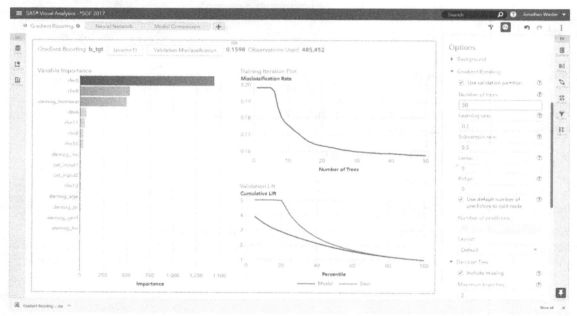

Figure 6. Interactive Gradient Boosting in SAS Visual Analytics

The next model we will build is a Neural Network, which is a statistical model that is designed to mimic the biological structures of the human brain that contains an input layer, multiple hidden layers, an output layer, and the connections between each of those.

Note that misclassification for the validation partition is 0.1970. The Network plot illustrates the relationship between your inputs and hidden layers. The next plot is the Iteration plot, which reports on the Objective/Loss function as the number of iterations increased. It appears that the Objective/Loss flattens around 20 iterations. You can tune the model further by changing the number of hidden layers, the number of neurons in each hidden layer, activation function for each layer, or other options.

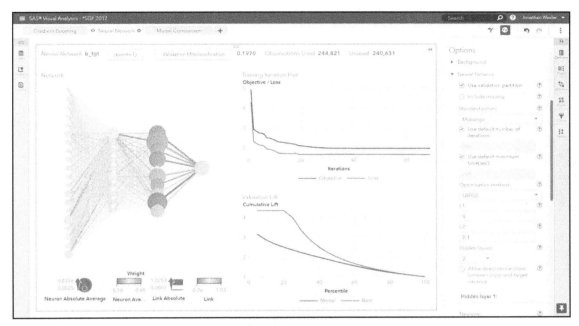

Figure 7. Interactive Two-Layer Neural Network in SAS Visual Analytics

The Model Comparison automatically chooses the best model based on the fit statistic selected in the Options panel. In this case, the model with the lowest misclassification rate is chosen. Note the partition, response, and event level much match across each model in order to generate the report. Gradient Boosting is selected as the champion model.

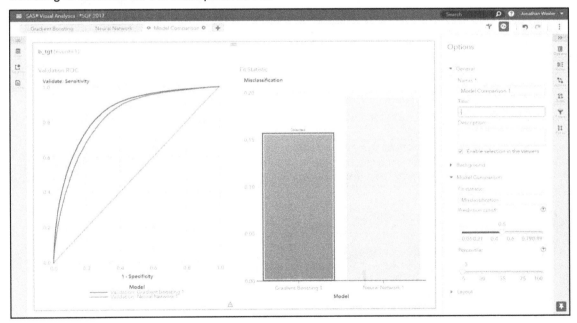

Figure 8. Interactive Model Comparison in SAS Visual Analytics

We will export the Gradient Boosting model so that it is accessible from SAS Studio in the next section. This model information will automatically be stored in the 'models' caslib as a binary analytic store (or astore) file.

Figure 9. Exporting Gradient Boosting Score Code from SAS Visual Analytics

BUILD MODELS PROGRAMATICALLY USING SAS STUDIO

Now that we have explored our data and built interactive models within SAS Visual Analytics to predict b_tgt, we might want to extend our analysis and build additional models within SAS Studio, our programmatic environment. Prior to building our models within SAS Visual Analytics, we created and promoted the BANK_PART CAS table to the public caslib so that it is available across multiple sessions and multiple users. In addition, this table contains a _partind_ variable to represent our training and validation partitions. The LIBNAME statement below points to this public caslib and allows the user within SAS Studio to build models with the same table that was loaded into memory and used to build our interactive models in SAS Visual Analytics.

```
libname mycaslib cas caslib=public;
```

The first step in our modeling process is to further "wrangle" our data. In this case, we have identified several predictors that have a high percentage of missing values. In order to address this, we will first run PROC VARIMPUTE to replace these missing values with the calculated mean of all of the nonmissing observations.

```
%let partitioned_data = mycaslib.bank_part;

proc varimpute data=&partitioned_data.;
  input demog_age demog_homeval demog_inc rfm3  /ctech=mean;
  output out=mycaslib.bank_prepped_temp copyvars=(_ALL_);
  code file="&outdir./impute_score.sas";
run;
```

Next, we might want to apply transformations to a few of the continuous predictors. These transformations can be done using in-memory SAS DATA step code. Notice that the data being used to build these transformations as well as the output table that is being created are both pointing to a caslib. When this is the case, the SAS DATA step code is run automatically in-memory without requiring any special requests. This table is then promoted with the PROMOTE=YES option so that it can be used later if we want to continue the model building process with these new variables in an environment such as Python. We will show this type of integration in the next section.

```
%let prepped_data = mycaslib.bank_prepped;
data &prepped_data (promote=YES);
  set mycaslib.bank_prepped_temp ;

  if (IM_RFM3 > 0) then LOG_IM_RFM3 = LOG(IM_RFM3);
  else LOG_IM_RFM3 = .;

  if (RFM1 > 0) then LOG_RFM1 = LOG(RFM1);
  else LOG_RFM1 = .;
run;
```

The first model we will build is a Decision Tree model. Decision Trees use a sequence of simple if-then-else rules to make a prediction or to classify an output. We will build this model with PROC TREESPLIT using the Entropy growing criterion and then apply the C45 methodology to select the optimal tree, which is based on the validation partition. We store the details of this tree model in the score code file treeselect_score.sas. This score code is applied to the bank data creating new columns that contain the predicted value for each observation.

```
/* Specify the data set inputs and target */
%let class_inputs    = cat_input1 cat_input2 demog_ho demog_genf
                       demog_genm;
%let interval_inputs = IM_demog_age IM_demog_homeval IM_demog_inc
                       demog_pr log_rfm1 rfm2 log_im_rfm3 rfm4-rfm12 ;
%let target          = b_tgt;

/* DECISION TREE predictive model                                  */
proc treesplit data=&prepped_data.;
  input &interval_inputs. / level=interval;
  input &class_inputs. / level=nominal;
  target &target. / level=nominal;
  partition rolevar=_partind_(train='1' validate='0');
  grow entropy;
  prune c45;
  code file="&outdir./treeselect_score.sas";
run;

/* Score the data using the generated tree model score code        */
data mycaslib._scored_tree;
  set &prepped_data.;
  %include "&outdir./treeselect_score.sas";
run;
```

In Figure 10, we see a partial tree diagram that was created from running PROC TREESPLIT. This shows that the first rule applied to the data was based on the predictor rfm5. Those observations that have a value for rfm5 that was less than or equal to 3.6 were passed into the left hand branch; those with a value of rfm5 that was greater than 3.6 were passed into the right hand branch. You can continue to follow the rules down the entire branch of a tree until arriving at the final node, which determines your classification.

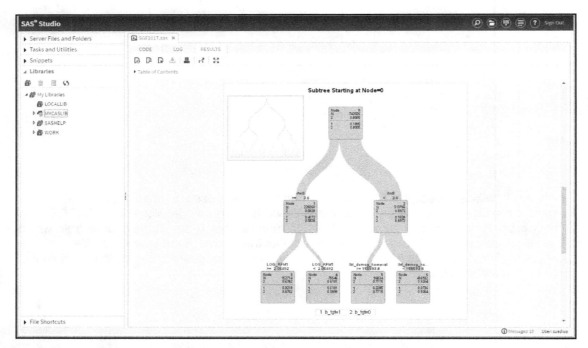

Figure 10. Decision Tree Subtree Diagram from SAS Studio

Note that the misclassification for the validation partition is 0.1447. The Variable Importance table reports the relative importance of all of the predictors that were used in building this model. We can see from this table that rfm5, LOG_RFM1, IM_demog_homeval, and rfm9 were the predictors that contributed the most in defining the splitting rules that made up this particular decision tree model.

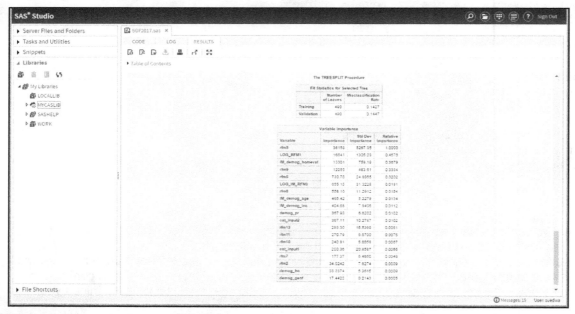

Figure 11. Decision Tree Fit Statistics and Variable Importance Metrics from SAS Studio

The next model that we will build is a Forest model. A Forest is an ensemble of individual trees where the final classification is based on an average of the probabilities across the trees that make up the forest. In many cases, finding the correct tuning parameters for a forest model can be quite tricky and time consuming. The autotuning options within PROC FOREST takes all of the guess work out of the tuning process and determines the optimal settings for these parameters based on the data. In this case, we allow PROC FOREST to autotune over the number of trees, the number of variables to try when splitting each node in the trees, and the in-bag fraction parameters for this model. We are using the outmodel option in this procedure to store all of the information about the model and to show an alternative to using score code. We can see mycaslib.forest_model being passed into the inmodel option within the second PROC FOREST call. This will be used to create our new output table containing our classifications for this model. Note that we could have specified the OUTPUT statement in the first PROC FOREST run because we are scoring the original input data. This approach would be used when you are scoring new data with the trained forest.

```
/* Autotune ntrees, vars_to_try and inbagfraction in Forest */
proc forest data=&prepped_data. intervalbins=20 minleafsize=5 seed=12345
outmodel=mycaslib.forest_model;
   input &interval_inputs. / level = interval;
   input &class_inputs. / level = nominal;
   target &target. / level=nominal;
   grow GAIN;
   partition rolevar=_partind_(train='1' validate='0');
   autotune maxiter=2 popsize=2 useparameters=custom
            tuneparms=(ntrees(lb=20 ub=100 init=100)
                       vars_to_try(init=5 lb=5 ub=20)
                       inbagfraction(init=0.6 lb=0.2 ub=0.9));
   ods output TunerResults=rf_tuner_results;
run;

/* Score the data using the generated Forest model */
proc forest data=&prepped_data. inmodel=mycaslib.forest_model noprint;
   output out=mycaslib._scored_FOREST copyvars=(b_tgt _partind_ account);
run;
```

In order to use this model in a different environment, such as in the next section where we use Python to build and compare models, the definition of this model must be promoted. For the Forest model, this definition was stored with the OUTMODEL option on the original PROC FOREST call creating the forest_model table. This promotion is done using PROC CASUTIL.

```
/* Promote the forest_model table */
proc casutil outcaslib="public" incaslib="public";
   promote casdata="forest_model";
quit;
```

Information about the autotuning process is shown in Figure 12. The Tuner Summary table details the optimization settings used to solve this problem. For example, the total tuning time of this model took 942.46 seconds with an Initial Objective Value of 7.3321 resulting in the Best Objective Value of 7.2532. The Best Configuration table shows that the optimal parameter settings for this data occurred at the second evaluation with 40 Trees, 11 Variables to Try, and a Bootstrap Sample (in-bag fraction) of 0.4027. Note that the misclassification for the validation partition is 0.0725.

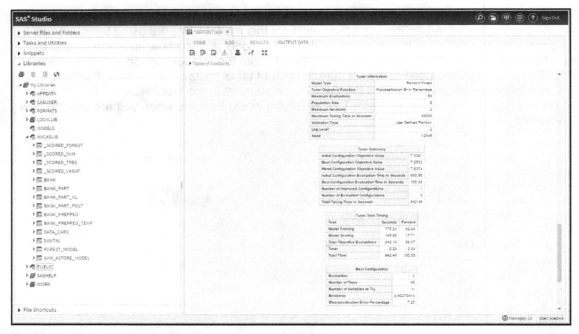

Figure 12. Forest Autotuning Metrics from SAS Studio

The final model that we will build is a Support Vector Machine. Support Vector Machines find a set of hyperplanes that best separate the levels of a binary target variable. We will use a polynomial kernel of degree 2 and store this complex model within a binary astore table called svm_astore_model. This table is then used in the PROC ASTORE call to generate the output table including your predicted classifications for this SVM model.

```
/* SUPPORT VECTOR MACHINE predictive model */
proc svmachine data=&prepped_data. (where=(_partind_=1));
   kernel polynom / deg=2;
   target &target. ;
   input &interval_inputs. / level=interval;
   input &class_inputs. / level=nominal;
   savestate rstore=mycaslib.svm_astore_model (promote=yes);
   ods exclude IterHistory;
run;

/* Score data using ASTORE code generated for the SVM model */
proc astore;
   score data=&prepped_data. out=mycaslib._scored_SVM
         rstore=mycaslib.svm_astore_model
         copyvars=(b_tgt _partind_ account);
run;

proc casutil outcaslib="public" incaslib="public";
   promote casdata="svm_astore_model";
quit;
```

Now that we have built several candidate models within SAS Studio, we want to compare these to each other to determine the best model for fitting this data. We also want to compare these with the original Gradient Boosting model, which was identified as the champion within SAS Visual Analytics. The details of this champion model were stored in an analytic store binary file and exported into the models library that is available within SAS Studio. To include this model in our comparisons, PROC ASTORE is run to apply this model to the BANK_PART data and to create the associated classifications.

14

```
proc casutil;
    Load casdata="Gradient_Boosting_VA.sashdat" incaslib="models"
    casout="gstate" outcaslib=casuser replace;
run;

data mycaslib.bank_part_post;
  set &partitioned_data.;
  _va_calculated_54_1=round('b_tgt'n,1.0);
  _va_calculated_54_2=round('demog_genf'n,1.0);
  _va_calculated_54_3=round('demog_ho'n,1.0);
  _va_calculated_54_4=round('_PartInd_'n,1.0);
run;

proc astore;
    score data=mycaslib.bank_part_post out=mycaslib._scored_vasgf
          rstore=casuser.gstate copyvars=(b_tgt _partind_ account ) ;
run;
```

These four candidate models are then passed to PROC ASSESS to calculate standard metrics including misclassification, lift, ROC, and more. Figure 13 shows that the best performing model for these candidates is the Forest model with a validation misclassification of 0.072532. This is also confirmed by looking at the ROC plot and the Lift values in the upper deciles.

```
/* Assess */
%macro assess_model(prefix=, var_evt=, var_nevt=);
  proc assess data=mycaslib._scored_&prefix.;
    input &var_evt.;
    target &target. / level=nominal event='1';
    fitstat pvar=&var_nevt. / pevent='0';
    by _partind_;

    ods output
      fitstat=&prefix._fitstat
      rocinfo=&prefix._rocinfo
      liftinfo=&prefix._liftinfo;
run;
%mend assess_model;

ods exclude all;
%assess_model(prefix=TREE, var_evt=p_b_tgt1, var_nevt=p_b_tgt0);
%assess_model(prefix=FOREST, var_evt=p_b_tgt1, var_nevt=p_b_tgt0);
%assess_model(prefix=SVM, var_evt=p_b_tgt1, var_nevt=p_b_tgt0);
%assess_model(prefix=VAGBM, var_evt=p_b_tgt1, var_nevt=p_b_tgt0);
ods exclude none;
```

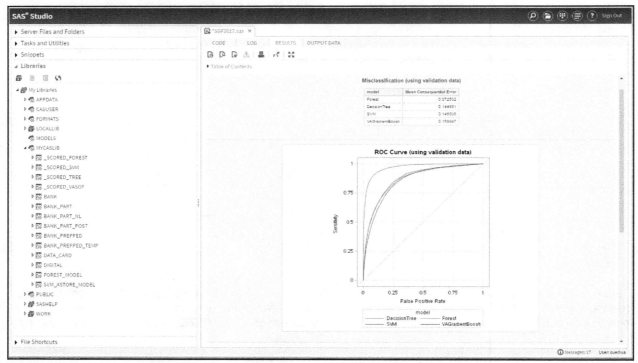

Figure 13. Assessment Statistics and ROC Curve for Candidate Models from SAS Studio

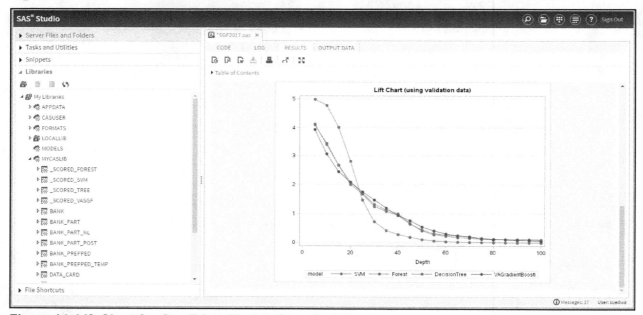

Figure 14. Lift Chart for Candidate Models from SAS Studio

BUILD MODEL PROGRAMMATICALLY USING PYTHON API

After exploring and modeling interactively in SAS Visual Analytics and programmatically in SAS Studio, we move into the open source world and finish this case study with another programmatic interface using the Python API. In this section, we will build a logistic regression model, score models that were built earlier in SAS Visual Analytics and SAS Studio, and compare them all to select a champion. The code and plots below are executed in Jupyter notebook.

16

We start by importing the SAS Scripting Wrapper for Analytics Transfer (SWAT) package to enable the connection and functionality of CAS. It is available at https://github.com/sassoftware/python-swat.

```
# Import packages
from swat import *
from pprint import pprint
from swat.render import render_html
from matplotlib import pyplot as plt
import pandas as pd
import sys
%matplotlib inline
```

The next step is to connect to CAS and start a new session. This step requires that you know the server host (cashost), port (casport), and authentication (casauth) of your CAS environment. Contact your SAS administrator for additional details and ensure that this code executes successfully before proceeding.

```
# Start a CAS session
cashost='cas_server_host.com'
casport=1234
casauth='~/_authinfo'
sess = CAS(cashost, casport, authinfo=casauth, caslib="public")
```

After execution, your CAS session can be accessed via the sess variable.

Next we define helper variables. Helper variables are those that are created in one place, at the beginning and reused afterward throughout the code. They include variables like the name of your input data set, its class and interval inputs, any shared caslibs, and so on.

```
# Set helper variables
gcaslib="public"
prepped_data="bank_prepped"
target = {"b_tgt"}
class_inputs = {"cat_input1", "cat_input2", "demog_ho", "demog_genf",
"demog_genm"}
interval_inputs = {"im_demog_age", "im_demog_homeval", "im_demog_inc",
"demog_pr", "log_rfm1", "rfm2", "log_im_rfm3", "rfm4", "rfm5", "rfm6",
"rfm7", "rfm8", "rfm9", "rfm10", "rfm11", "rfm12"}
class_vars = target | class_inputs
```

We begin by building a logistic regression model with stepwise selection, using the same set of inputs and target (b_tgt) used in the SAS Studio interface. Logistic regression models a binary target (0 or 1) and computes probabilities of the target event (1) as a function of specified inputs. This model uses the training partition of BANK_PREPPED table that was created and promoted to public caslib in SAS Studio. Because the table is promoted, it is available to any session on CAS, including ours.

After the model is run, the parameter estimates, fit statistics, and so on are displayed using render_html function from swat.render package. The Selection Summary in Figure 15 below lists the order of input variables selected at each step based on the SBC criterion. The misclassification rate for the validation partition is 0.1569. Finally, the predicted probabilities p_b_tgt0 and p_b_tgt1 are created using SAS DATA step code through the dataStep.runCode CAS action – these are needed later when invoking the model assessment function asses_model.

Note: Before invoking any CAS action, make sure the appropriate CAS actionset is loaded using sess.loadactionset. In the code below, notice that the regression actionset is loaded before the logistic action is invoked.

```
# Load action set
sess.loadactionset(actionset="regression")
```

```
# Train Logistic Regression
lr=sess.regression.logistic(
  table={"name":prepped_data, "caslib":gcaslib},
  classVars=[{"vars":class_vars}],
  model={
    "depVars":[{"name":"b_tgt", "options":{"event":"1"}}],
    "effects":[{"vars":class_inputs | interval_inputs}]
  },
  partByVar={"name":"_partind_", "train":"1", "valid":"0"},
  selection={"method":"STEPWISE"},
  output={"casOut":{"name":"_scored_logistic", "replace":True},
"copyVars":{"account", "b_tgt", "_partind_"}}
)

# Output model statistics
render_html(lr)

# Compute p_b_tgt0 and p_b_tgt1 for assessment
sess.dataStep.runCode(
  code="data _scored_logistic; set _scored_logistic; p_b_tgt0=1-_pred_;
rename _pred_=p_b_tgt1; run;"
)
```

Selection Summary					
Step	Effect Entered	Effect Removed	Number Of Effects	SBC	Optimal SBC
0	Intercept		1	736748.2097	0
1	rfm5		2	635388.82523	0
2	IM_demog_homeval		3	602525.74866	0
3	LOG_RFM1		4	565460.62424	0
4	rfm9		5	528458.08771	0
5	rfm12		6	525332.71656	0
6	cat_input1		7	523914.11582	0
7	cat_input2		8	522798.02005	0
8	rfm4		9	522395.70936	1

Figure 15. Selection Summary of Logistic Regression Model from Python API

After building a model using the Python API, let us score few models created in SAS Visual Analytics and SAS Studio to understand how a model created in one interface can be shared and reused in another. We will begin with the Gradient Boosting model created in SAS Visual DATA steps. When this model was built, it produced two artifacts: SAS data step code and an astore file that was saved to models caslib.

To score the Gradient Boosting model using these artifacts, the code does the following:
1. Loads the astore file into a local user caslib (casuser)
2. Runs SAS DATA step code created in SAS Visual Analytics – this transforms the input data set BANK_PREPPED with any necessary changes made within this interface
3. Scores the transformed input data set (from step 2) using the loaded astore file (from step 1) that contains model parameters
4. Renames predicted probability variable names for assessment

```
# 1. Load GBM model (ASTORE) created in VA
sess.loadTable(
  caslib="models", path="Gradient_Boosting_VA.sashdat",
  casout={"name":"gbm_astore_model","caslib":"casuser", "replace":True}
)

# 2. Score code from VA (for data preparation)
sess.dataStep.runCode(
  code="""data bank_part_post;
          set bank_part(caslib='public');
          _va_calculated_54_1=round('b_tgt'n,1.0);
          _va_calculated_54_2=round('demog_genf'n,1.0);
          _va_calculated_54_3=round('demog_ho'n,1.0);
          _va_calculated_54_4=round('_PartInd_'n,1.0);
        run;"""
)

# 3. Score using ASTORE
sess.loadactionset(actionset="astore")

sess.astore.score(
  table={"name":"bank_part_post"},
  rstore={"name":"gbm_astore_model"},
  out={"name":"_scored_gbm", "replace":True},
  copyVars={"account", "_partind_", "b_tgt"}
)

# 4. Rename p_b_tgt0 and p_b_tgt1 for assessment
sess.dataStep.runCode(
  code="""data _scored_gbm;
          set _scored_gbm;
          rename p__va_calculated_54_10=p_b_tgt0
                 p__va_calculated_54_11=p_b_tgt1;
        run;"""
)
```

We repeat the scoring process with the autotuned Forest model created in SAS Studio. Remember that this model was saved earlier as a CAS table called forest_model in the public caslib. Here the decisionTree.forestScore action scores the input data set BANK_PREPPED using the forest_model table. The SAS DATA step that follows creates the necessary predicted probability variable names for assessment.

```
# Load action set
sess.loadactionset(actionset="decisionTree")

# Score using forest_model table
sess.decisionTree.forestScore(
  table={"name":prepped_data, "caslib":gcaslib},
  modelTable={"name":"forest_model", "caslib":"public"},
  casOut={"name":"_scored_rf", "replace":True},
  copyVars={"account", "b_tgt", "_partind_"},
  vote="PROB"
)
```

```
# Create p_b_tgt0 and p_b_tgt1 as _rf_predp_ is the probability of event in
_rf_predname_
sess.dataStep.runCode(
  code="""data _scored_rf;
          set _scored_rf;
          if _rf_predname_=1 then do;
            p_b_tgt1=_rf_predp_;
            p_b_tgt0=1-p_b_tgt1;
          end;
          if _rf_predname_=0 then do;
            p_b_tgt0=_rf_predp_;
            p_b_tgt1=1-p_b_tgt0;
          end;
        run;"""
)
```

Lastly we score the Support Vector Machine model created in SAS Studio using the analytic store (astore) table svm_astore_model located in public caslib.

```
# Score using ASTORE
sess.loadactionset(actionset="astore")

sess.astore.score(
  table={"name":prepped_data, "caslib":gcaslib},
  rstore={"name":"svm_astore_model", "caslib":"public"},
  out={"name":"_scored_svm", "replace":True},
  copyVars={"account", "_partind_", "b_tgt"}
)
```

The final step in the case study is to assess and compare all of the models that were created and scored, including both the interactively and programmatically created models. The assessment is based on the validation partition of the data. The code below uses the percentile.assess action for Logistic Regression model but similar code can be used to generate assessments for all other models.

```
# Assess models
def assess_model(prefix):
    return sess.percentile.assess(
      table={
        "name":"_scored_" + prefix,
        "where": "strip(put(_partind_, best.))='0'"
      },
      inputs=[{"name":"p_b_tgt1"}],
      response="b_tgt",
      event="1",
      pVar={"p_b_tgt0"},
      pEvent={"0"}
    )

lrAssess=assess_model(prefix="logistic")
lr_fitstat =lrAssess.FitStat
lr_rocinfo =lrAssess.ROCInfo
lr_liftinfo=lrAssess.LIFTInfo
```

To choose a champion, we will use the ROC and Lift plots. Figures 16 and 17 shows that the autotuned Forest (SAS Studio) is the winner compared to the Logistic Regression (Python API), Support Vector

Machine (SAS Studio) and Gradient Boosting (SAS Visual Analytics) models as it has higher lift and more area under the ROC curve.

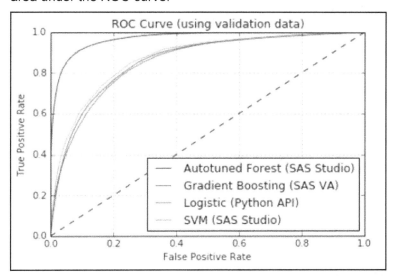

Figure 16. ROC Chart for Candidate Models

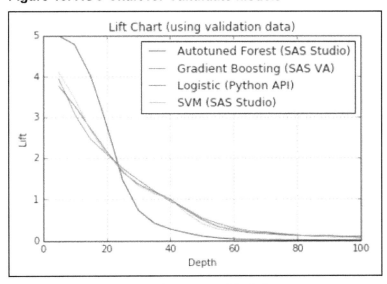

Figure 17. Lift Chart for Candidate Models

The goal of this case study is to highlight the unified and open architecture of SAS Viya -- how models built across various interfaces (SAS Visual Analytics, SAS Studio, and Python API) can seamlessly access data sets and intermediary results and easily score across them. Now that you understand the basics, you can build the best predictive model possible.

CONCLUSION

As previously stated, you should be able to solve business problems using your tool *and* method of choice, with no technological limitations. As shown in this paper, you can interactively build models quickly and accurately, and continue your analysis programmatically, without sacrificing inaccuracy from inefficient manual handoffs.

SAS Viya enables you to explore your data deeper, using the latest innovations in in-memory analytics. SAS is committed to delivering new, innovative data mining and machine learning algorithms that will scale to the size of your business, now and in the future.

REFERENCES

Koch, P., Wujek, B., Golovidov, O., and Gardner, S. (2017). "Automated Hyperparameter Tuning for Effective Machine Learning." In *Proceedings of the SAS Global Forum 2017 Conference*. Cary, NC: SAS Institute Inc.

ACKNOWLEDGMENTS

The authors express sincere gratitude to the SAS® Visual Data Mining and Machine Learning developers, testers, and also to our customers.

RECOMMENDED READING AND ASSETS

- SAS Visual Analytics, SAS Visual Statistics, and SAS Visual Data Mining and Machine Learning 8.1 on SAS Viya: Video Library (Visual)
  http://support.sas.com/training/tutorial/viyava/

- SAS Visual Data Mining and Machine Learning on SAS Viya: Video Library (Programming)
  http://support.sas.com/training/tutorial/viya/index.html

- SAS Visual Data Mining and Machine Learning Fact Sheet
  http://www.sas.com/content/dam/SAS/en_us/doc/factsheet/sas-visual-data-mining-machine-learning-1082751.pdf

- SAS Visual Data Mining and Machine Learning Community
  https://communities.sas.com/t5/SAS-Visual-Data-Mining-and/bd-p/dmml

- SAS Viya Documentation
  http://support.sas.com/documentation/onlinedoc/viya/

- SAS Software Github Page
  https://github.com/sassoftware

CONTACT INFORMATION

Your comments and questions are valued and encouraged. Contact the author at:

Jonathan Wexler
SAS Institute Inc.
100 SAS Campus Drive
Cary, NC 27513
Email: jonathan.wexler@sas.com

Susan Haller
SAS Institute Inc.
100 SAS Campus Drive
Cary, NC 27513
Email: susan.haller@sas.com

Radhikha Myneni
SAS Institute Inc.
100 SAS Campus Drive
Cary, NC 27513
Email: radhikha.myneni@sas.com

Interactive Modeling in SAS® Visual Analytics

Don Chapman, SAS Institute Inc.

ABSTRACT

SAS® Visual Analytics has two add-on offerings, SAS® Visual Statistics and SAS® Visual Data Mining and Machine Learning, that provide knowledge workers and data scientists an interactive interface for data partition, data exploration, feature engineering, and rapid modeling. These offerings are powered by the SAS® Viya™ platform, thus enabling big data and big analytic problems to be solved. This paper focuses on the steps a user would perform during an interactive modeling session.

INTRODUCTION

This paper illustrates how the use of the highly interactive, visual SAS Visual Data Mining and Machine Learning offering will not only make your data problems manageable but also engaging. This offering is composed of capabilities that range from data preparation to programmatic access to advanced machine learning in your language of choice. Each capability in the offering would require its own paper to do it justice, so this paper focuses on integrated data exploration, reporting, and analytical modeling. SAS® Visual Analytics allows collaboration between business analysts, citizen data scientists, and data scientists. This is important because the data scientists apply analytical methods to business data to create insights that drive the business direction.

This paper and the associated presentation will focus on the case study of a day in the life of a data scientist who needs to solve a business problem quickly. How do they acquire the data and get it prepared for modeling? How do they explore the data to understand its characteristics? How do they generate and compare models? How do they document those insights and apply them to solving a business problem?

THE BUSINESS PROBLEM

Picture yourself pulling into Starbucks on the way to work. Your manager calls to tell you that she has to pitch a plan to increase profits by 5% this year. She needs you to put together her presentation for an executive meeting tomorrow afternoon. This unfortunately is how too many of your days start. An unplanned request just became your top priority.

Time for a little background. You are a data scientist at the Insight Toy Company who works closely with a vice president of sales and marketing. Sales to our vendors have been slowly declining for the last couple of years and your manager has been asked to increase profits in her organization by 5% this year. It's time to get Insight Toy back on track.

THE PLAN

The first thing you need to do is come up with a plan for tackling this challenging task. Fortunately for you, Insight Toy has been collecting data for several years on all aspects of the business. They also have a great IT department who prepares the data for its analysts and data scientists. A quick inventory of the corporate data shows that you have access to the last two years of sales data. This data includes information on what products are sold to which vendors, the costs associated with the order, along with some metrics about the sales representative and the vendor.

Step one, come up with a plan. You decide to follow the tried-and-true strategy of:

1. Review the data and make a quick exploratory pass over the most relevant variables to understand their characteristics and relationships

2. Feature engineering

3. Start generating models and reviewing their results

4.   Compare your models, and come up with a champion

5.   Validate your model and apply it

6.   Come up with a couple of potential solutions and present them to your manager

REVIEW AND EXPLORE THE DATA

Exploring the data is an important step in understanding the relationships within. A quick pass over the data and you see that you have the entire order history for every vendor dating back to January 1st, 2015. The first task you tackle is to look at the shape and characteristics of Order Profit, your response variable.

Next you want to see if there are any linear correlations between Order Profit and other variables you think contribute to Insight Toy's profit. You create a page and add a correlation matrix, as shown in Figure 1, to investigate the relationships. It reveals that Order Amount has a strong correlation as you would expect. Two other variables, Amount Returned and Vendor Satisfaction have a moderate correlation. You immediately document your findings by adding a comment to the report stating your observations.

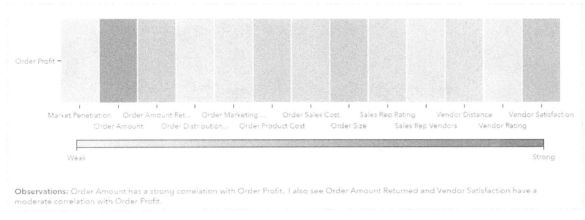

Observations: Order Amount has a strong correlation with Order Profit. I also see Order Amount Returned and Vendor Satisfaction have a moderate correlation with Order Profit.

Figure 1. Correlation of Order Profit to Key Variables

The advantage you have in solving today's challenge is that you are using SAS Visual Analytics. This application has integrated data exploration, modeling, and reporting capabilities in a highly visual and interactive user interface. What else can the data tell you?

One the same page you add a List Table. A trusty table can convey a lot of information, especially when it aggregates the data for you. Figure 2 shows the aggregated list table you created.

Vendor Region	Vendor Type	Product Line	Order Amount	Order Amount Returned ▼	Vendor Satisfaction
West	Discount Store	Game	$1,064,183	$483,422	52%
West	Discount Store	Figure	$954,058	$459,535	52%
Midwest	Discount Store	Game	$668,794	$374,176	50%
Midwest	Discount Store	Figure	$655,808	$372,329	50%
Northeast	Discount Store	Figure	$725,401	$367,407	52%
Northeast	Discount Store	Game	$738,512	$347,149	52%
South	Discount Store	Game	$526,503	$323,783	49%
Northeast	Discount Store	Bead	$596,938	$311,516	52%
West	Convenience Store	Bead	$511,971	$300,135	51%
South	Discount Store	Figure	$455,788	$280,971	49%
Midwest	Discount Store	Bead	$530,831	$278,477	50%
West	Discount Store	Plush	$577,147	$275,090	53%

Observation: When you sort Order Amount Returned descending you see Discount Store vendors with a low Vendor Satisfaction are at the top of the list.

Figure 2. Returns List

You quickly see that the Vendor Type and Vendor Satisfaction need further investigation. The eyeball test shows that Discount Stores have the highest dollar amount for returns and you also see that vendor satisfaction is low for the vendors making returns.

On the next page you pull together several charts to quickly visualize the data. These charts, as seen in Figure 3, show you that convenience stores are also troublesome with respect to returns. They also show you that Product Line does not appear to be related to the returns.

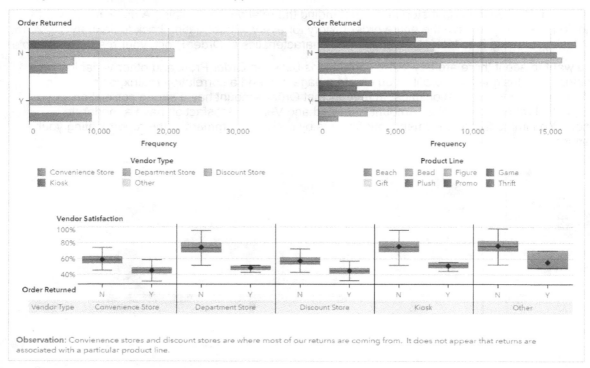

Figure 3. Returns Charts

You now understand the data better and have a good idea that decreasing the number of returned orders will help the bottom line.

Next you want to see what it will take to increase profits by 5%. A quick forecast, as shown in Figure 4, shows you that going after those returns will help Insight Toy's bottom line. You are happy to see the forecasting algorithm takes into account the seasonality of your products.

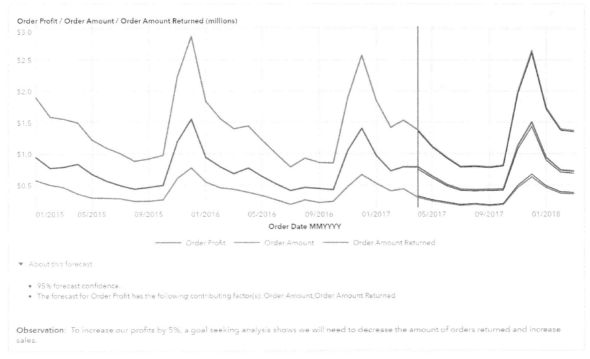

Figure 4. Profit Forecast

You used what-if analysis, specifically goal seeking as shown in Figure 5, to create this forecast. You can clearly see that Order Amount, which is how much our sales team is selling, needs to increase slightly in addition to the decrease in the amount of orders returned.

Figure 5. Goal Seeking

FEATURE ENGINEERING

As a data scientist you need to engineer features using your domain knowledge of Insight Toy and the problem at hand. SAS Visual Statistics and SAS Visual Data Mining and Machine Learning support traditional feature engineering such as segmentation. Calculations and custom categories are two features you can interactively create using a drag-and-drop interface or by editing code. You can create calculations based on simple math, for example here is the code for Order Profit:

```
( 'Order Amount'n - 'Order Amount Returned'n ) - 'Order Total Cost'n
```

You can also create calculations with conditional statements, for example Figure 6 shows the Vendor Active calculation in the calculation editor:

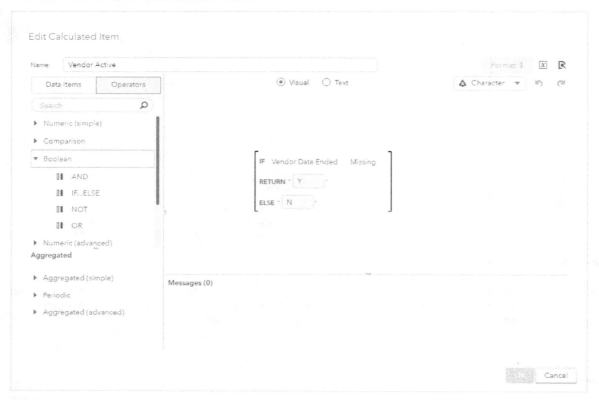

Figure 6. Calculation Editor

You also have the power to create ad-hoc hierarchies on-the-fly, duplicate a variable and change its format or aggregation, and even convert a measure to a category. The Order Date MMYYY data item shown in Figure 7 was created by duplicating the Order Date data item and changing its format.

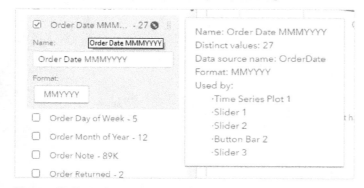

Figure 7. Data Item

Some algorithms, such as a linear regression, assume the data comes from a normal distribution. You take a quick look at the shape and distribution of your data since you are interested in Order Amount Returned. The two graphs on the left side of Figure 8 show that the Order Amount Returned variable is right-skewed.

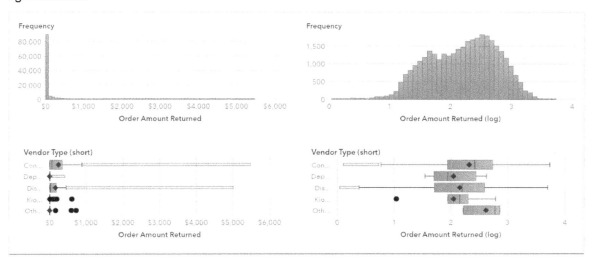

Figure 8. Variable Transformation

A log transformation can easily be created to reduce skewness. The code for the Order Amount Returned (log) calculation is:

```
( 'Order Amount Returned'n Log 10 )
```

The two graphs on the right side of Figure 8 show that the Order Amount Returned (log) variable follows a more normal distribution.

All calculations are dynamically constructed when the report is opened. This means you do not need to save a copy of the data for every report you create.

MODEL, MODEL, MODEL

Now it is time to start modeling. You know you have a binary response of either Y(es) or N(o) for Order Returned, so good candidate models are logistic regression, decision tree, forest, gradient boosting, neural network, and support vector machine. You want to model the vendors who have an event of Y; they are the ones returning orders.

The corporate data source has a partition variable that will allow you to train your models against a subset of the data and validate it against the rest of the data. By using partioning, you will generate the best models without overtraining.

You decide to start out with a tried-and-true logistic regression model using data on the four costs associated with the order, information about the vendor, and the product line as your effect variables. In less than a minute you interactively add the model to the report, assign the response and effect variables, and configure modeling options.

The model shown in Figure 9 looks good. You can see a summary of how well the effect variables fit, the distribution of your residuals, and the model's misclassification chart. While the default statistic is the validation misclassification, you can also look at a number of other statistics such as AIC or R-Square.

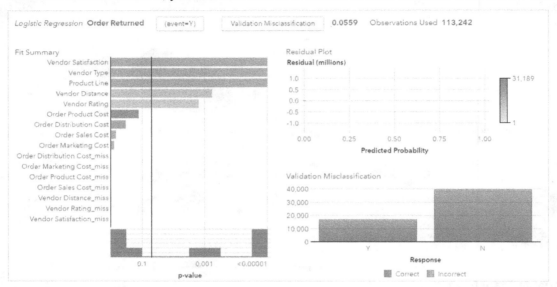

Figure 9. Logistic Regression

With a click of the mouse, you easily switch the validation misclassification chart to a validation lift chart, as shown in Figure 10, and then a validation ROC chart, as shown in Figure 11.

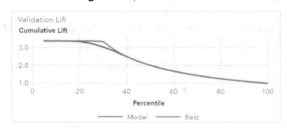

Figure 10. Logistic Regression Lift Chart   **Figure 11. Logistic Regression ROC Chart**

You use the same response and effects / target variables for creating additional models. On individual pages you create a decision tree model, forest model, gradient boosting model, neural network model, and support vector machine model. Each of these models is helping you predicted whether a vendor will return an order. The pages containing each of these models are shown in Figure 12 - Figure 16.

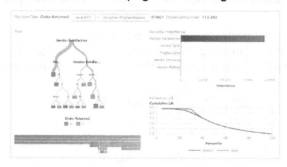

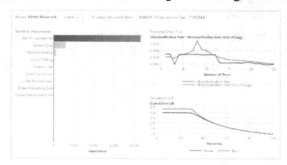

Figure 12. Decision Tree   **Figure 13. Forest**

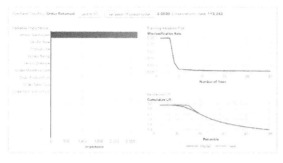

Figure 14. Gradient Boosting

Figure 15. Neural Network

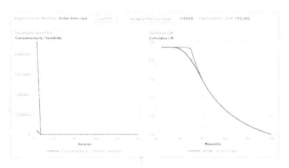

Figure 16. Support Vector Machine

As you create each model, you notice that Vendor Satisfaction is consistently one of the most important predictors for when an order is returned. You make a mental note of this observation.

MODEL COMPARISON

Once all the models are created, you can quickly compare all six in the model comparison visualization shown in Figure 17. There are fourteen different fit statistics that can be used to help you determine the champion model. The application guides you through this process by displaying the selected / best model for the active fit statistic.

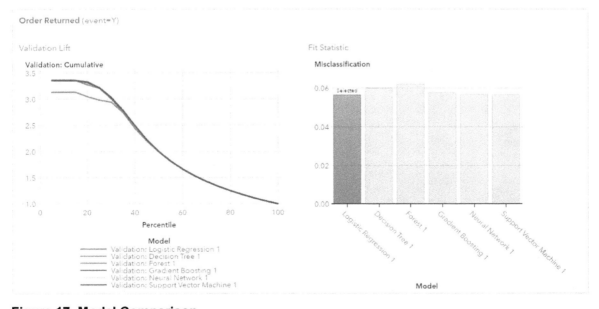

Figure 17. Model Comparison

After reviewing several of the fit statistics, you decide the logistic regression model is your champion. Don't forget to annotate the model comparison page with information on how and why you choose this model as the champion.

INTERACTIVELY REVIEW THE MODEL

This is where the power of having an interactive modeling tool pays dividends. You flip back to the page with your champion model, the logistic regression, and with a click of the mouse you derive the predicted value and probability value for the model. These values, Probability: Order Returned=Y and Predicted: Order Returned, are now available as new data items in the report. This allows you to use them as inputs to other models or as data items in report visuals. The data items for the logistic regression are stored as score code in the report. You also have the option to export the model for use in other applications such as SAS® Studio or to place it in your corporate analytics process.

Time to review our objective: you need to come up with a plan to increase profits by 5% this year. You have narrowed down options to reducing the amount of orders returned by Insight Toy vendors. You have modeled the vendors who have returned orders. Next you review the model to see if you can segment the vendors for a campaign targeted at the vendors that are returning the most orders.

You decide to review the model's prediction for Order Returned. You create a page, see Figure 18, that allows you to visualize the actual number of orders returned and the predicted number of orders returned based on the Probability Order Returned=Y. This page includes a parameter to dynamically control the prediction cutoff to review different scenarios.

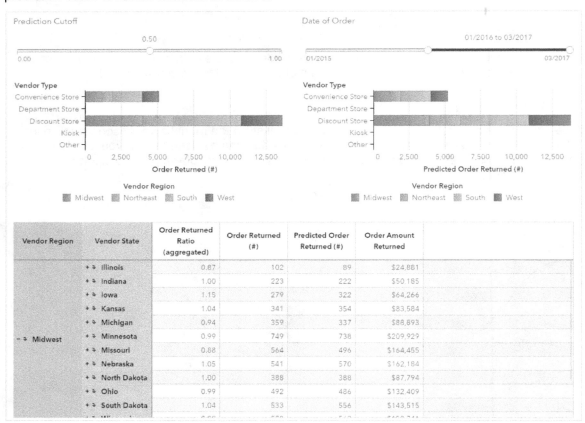

Figure 18. Model Review

You review the results of your logistic regression model and you feel good about its ability to help you predict which vendors are returning orders.

You have two analytics that are perfect for segmentation: k-means clustering and decision tree. You use clustering to segment based on Probability Order Returned=Y and Vendor Satisfaction. You are using the results of your logistic regression model, Probability Order Returned=Y, as a cluster input variable. The other input variable, Vendor Satisfaction, was consistently one of the most important predictors identified during modeling. Figure 19 shows the results of your segmentation.

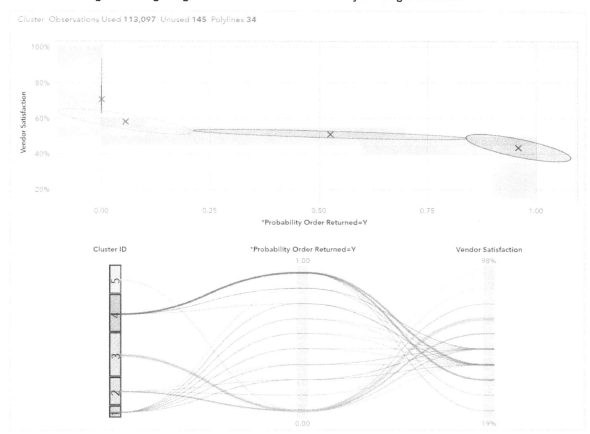

Figure 19. K-Means Clustering

You can interactively change the view in the parallel coordinates plot, as show in Figure 20. You observe from the parallel coordinates plot that the highest probability for an order to be returned is with cluster 4 and there is some contribution from cluster 1. You also observe that they have low vendor satisfaction, which aligns with everything you have seen so far.

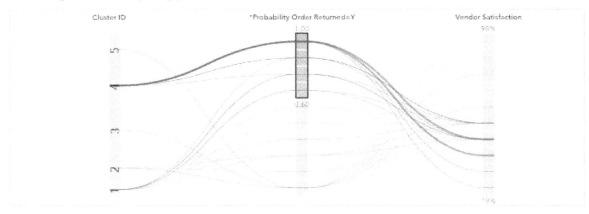

Figure 20. Clustering Parallel Coordinates Plot

You easily derive the clusters from the visualization and generate a new feature, Targeted Vendors – Cluster, to help you solve your business problem.

Next you want to visualize the results of your cluster-based segmentation by using Targeted Vendors – Cluster. Figure 21 shows a highly interactive set of visualizations that allow you to filter the entire page by Vendor Region and Order Date. It also allows you to only display a specified number of top vendors. On this page you applied a filter to show information about the Midwest starting in January of last year. At the bottom of the page is a stacked container that allows you to view details on the amount and number of orders returned.

Figure 21. Cluster Targeted Vendors – Geographic

The stacked container allows you to navigate from the Geo Map view shown at the bottom of Figure 21 to the Vendor Type view show in Figure 22.

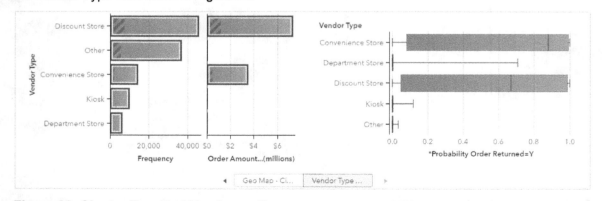

Figure 22. Cluster Targeted Vendors – Type

11

The Vendor Type view shows you what percentage of the data for each Vendor Type comes from what is displayed in the butterfly chart. It also shows you a box plot of the probability an order was returned by the type of vendor.

Next you use a decision tree to segment Predicted: Order Returned based on Product Line, Vendor Type, Vendor Satisfaction, and Vendor State. Similar to the clustering segmentation, you are using the results of your logistic regression model, Predicted: Order Returned, as your response variable in your segmentation. Figure 23 shows the results of your segmentation.

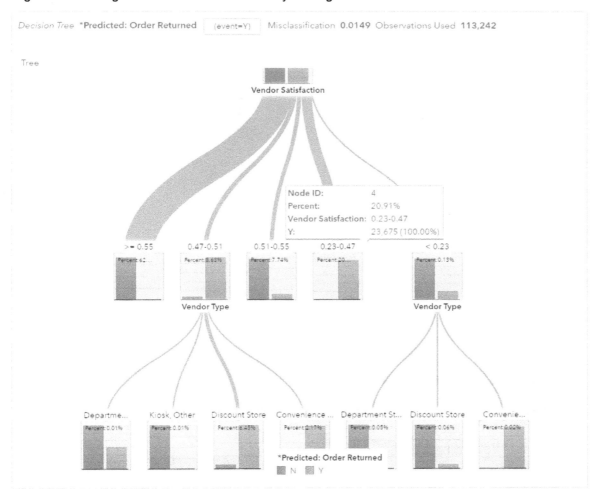

Figure 23. Decision Tree Segmentation

You observe from the decision tree that one node, the fourth one in from the left on the second level, has the highest percentage of Y(es) observations for Predicted: Order Returned. You easily derive the decision tree node IDs from the visualization and generate a new feature, Targeted Vendors – DTree, to provide a second segment to help you solve your business problem.

To compare the two features you have created, you visualize the results of your decision tree based segmentation by using Targeted Vendors – DTree in the same type of visualization you used for Targeted Vendors – Cluster. Figure 24 and Figure 25 show these visualizations.

Figure 24. DTree Targeted Vendors – Geographic

From these results you confirm that node 4 has the largest contribution to Order Amount Returned.

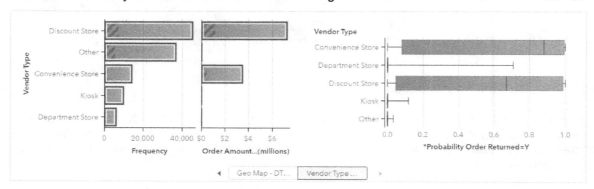

Figure 25. DTree Targeted Vendors - Type

13

Now it's time to put your analytics on the line and make your manager look good. With some additional feature engineering you have constructed a page for the cluster proposal and a page for the decision tree proposal. Each page allows you to enter one or two segments and a targeted return rate for every sales office. Based on this information, a bar chart will dynamically show you how the actual profits and projected profits would compare to the targeted profits for each quarter over the last couple of years. A set of donut charts will dynamically update to show you how many vendors need to be contacted in each state.

Figure 26 shows you the cluster proposal.

Figure 26. Cluster Proposal

You enter cluster 4, the segment containing the majority of the orders returned, and a value of 30 for the targeted reduction in return rate. The reduction in return rate specifies the percentage of returns that need to be eliminated. If the sales organization can reduce returns by 30%, then Insight Toy would have seen profits exceed the target for every quarter but one.

The donut chart at the bottom of the page shows you the vendors that should be targeted for this campaign. There are 1,215 vendors to contact and 7,727 that do not need to be contacted. The state that has the most vendors to contact is Texas, and it has 152. In addition to the overall visualization for projected vendors to contact, you can navigate to targeted donut chart based on Vendor Type.

Figure 27 shows you the decision tree proposal with the same visualizations as the cluster proposal.

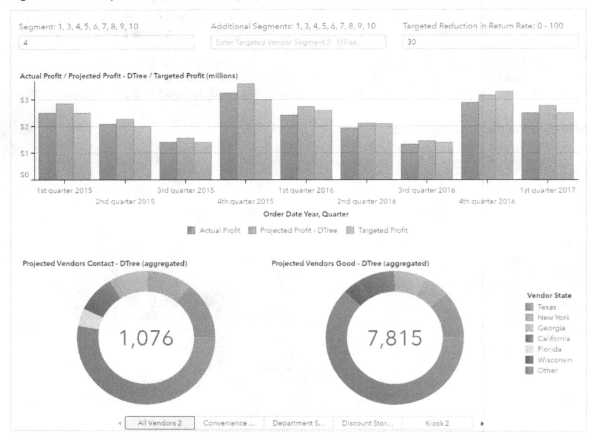

Figure 27. DTree Proposal

You enter node 4, the segment containing the majority of the orders returned, and a value of 30 for the targeted reduction in return rate. The results for the decision tree proposal are similar to those for the cluster proposal. One difference between the proposals is that fewer vendors need to be contacted for the decision tree proposal.

The stacked container at the bottom of the page also contains a list table with details on the vendors that need to be contacted. In Figure 28 you sorted the list by Order Amount Returned. Your sales organization can access this report to determine which vendors they need to contact. They can also export the list to a spreadsheet.

Vendor State	Vendor City	Vendor	Vendor Type	Vendor Satisfaction	*Probability Order Returned=Y	Order Amount Returned ▼
New Hampshire	Manchester	vend:000044FG	Discount Store	42%	0.98	$151,887
New Hampshire	Manchester	vend:000044FK	Discount Store	44%	0.95	$139,035
North Dakota	Bismarck	vend:00000NET	Discount Store	44%	0.98	$104,827
South Dakota	Pierre	vend:00000LKK	Discount Store	43%	0.99	$86,322
New Hampshire	Manchester	vend:000045OD	Convenience Store	51%	0.63	$81,246
Massachusetts	Worcester	vend:00003UUJ	Discount Store	45%	0.95	$80,484
South Dakota	Pierre	vend:00000KMJ	Discount Store	46%	0.95	$76,829
New Hampshire	Manchester	vend:000044FH	Discount Store	49%	0.65	$75,467
Nevada	Reno	vend:00000O69	Convenience Store	46%	0.97	$75,186
South Dakota	Pierre	vend:00000IU5	Discount Store	47%	0.89	$74,142
Connecticut	Hartford	vend:00003YI4	Discount Store	49%	0.67	$71,280
Washington	Olympia	vend:00000LNC	Discount Store	46%	0.80	$70,504

◀ Department S... Discount Stor... Kiosk 2 Other 2 Contact List 2 ▶

Figure 28. Contact List

You have a solid proposal with two options to present to your manager. The proposal is to get the sales offices to increase sales, but more importantly work with their vendors to decrease the number of orders returned. One aspect of the sales/vendor relationship that contributes to orders being returned is dissatisfied vendors. The sales team needs to engage the vendors to increase satisfaction.

Your work will help turn Insight Toy into a profitable company again.

CONCLUSION

The SAS Visual Statistics and SAS Visual Data Mining and Machine Learning add-on offerings to SAS Visual Analytics contain a robust set of tools that allow data scientists to explore their data, engineer features, interactively generate models, and use the model's output all within the same report. The integration of advanced modeling techniques, approachable analytics, and reporting capabilities provide the data scientist with a single tool for solving complex business problems and presenting the results in a business-friendly format.

CONTACT INFORMATION

Your comments and questions are valued and encouraged. Contact the author at:

Don Chapman
SAS Institute Inc.
Don.Chapman@sas.com

Paper SAS0747-2017

Open Your Mind: Use Cases for SAS® and Open-Source Analytics

Tuba Islam, SAS Institute Inc.

ABSTRACT

Data scientists need analytical tools and algorithms, whether commercial or open source, and will always have some favourites. But how do you decide when to use what? And how can you integrate their use to your maximum advantage? This paper provides best practices for deploying both SAS® and open-source analytical tools to increase productivity and efficiency in your enterprise ecosystem. Further, an example is provided of an analytical business flow for marketing using SAS and R algorithms in SAS® Enterprise Miner™ for developing a predictive model, and then operationalizing and automating that model for scoring, performance monitoring and retraining. There are also suggestions for using Python and SAS integration in a Jupyter Notebook environment. Seeing these examples will help you decide how to improve your analytics with similar integration of SAS and open source.

INTRODUCTION

This paper provides you with some examples to show the goodness of using open source and SAS in an enterprise ecosystem. Working in an open environment with various tools brings some challenges. It sometimes becomes more difficult to execute models in production quickly without extensive recoding. It can also become more challenging to automate the complete business flow for model management and to enable governance and lineage for analytics. SAS provides the analytical platform that connects the dots in the model lifecycle and helps "productionize" open-source models.

Some of the main benefits of SAS and open source working together:

- Freedom to use your language of choice as a data scientist, work collaboratively, and be able to exchange the resources and the analytical assets within the organization.
- Operationalize and automate the execution of your open source and SAS models in production quickly and increase the value gained from analytics.
- A transparent and easy-to-monitor analytical process and the governance and lineage for your models.

You will find an example of a campaign propensity use case in SAS® 9.4 using SAS® Enterprise Miner™ and SAS® Decision Manager for operationalizing open source R models and also the use of Jupyter notebook for accessing these models via REST and running post analysis in Python.

PREREQUISITES

For R integration on SAS 9.4, you will need to install R and the required packages on the server where SAS Enterprise Miner resides and set the required environment parameters such as R_HOME and RLANG. The details for the installation and configuration can be found on SAS Communities portal when you search for R integration.

For Python integration on SAS 9.4, you will need to install Python and SASPy package to execute SAS code in Jupyter Notebook. The package and the instructions can be found under SASPy repository on GitHub. For Python integration on SAS® Viya™, you would install the package in python-swat repository on GitHub. This paper will only include examples for SAS 9.4.

STEP-BY-STEP ANALYTICS WITH SAS AND OPEN SOURCE

You will find the analytical steps of a marketing use case that builds a campaign propensity model for buying an organic product using SAS and open-source analytics. Open Source Integration node in SAS Enterprise Miner will be used for creating R models and making them production-ready. The use case will include one-click registration of models into SAS Decision Manager with the unique model ID that will enable the business users to track the performance of campaign models in production.

The marketing data includes customer demographics and historical purchase information about different products. The purchase event is flagged as 1/0 and stored in the variable called "Target". The sample dataset and the code snippets shared in the paper are available on GitHub under enlighten-integration repository.

STEP 1. BUILD PRODUCTION MODELS IN SAS® ENTERPRISE MINER™

The Open Source Integration node enables the execution of R code within SAS Enterprise Miner. This node transfers the data, the metadata, and the results automatically between two systems. It facilitates multitasking in R by running models in parallel. The Open Source Integration node enables certain R models to be translated into SAS DATA step code and deployed in production.

The default setting for the output mode in the Open Source Integration node is "PMML", which is an open standard. The R models that are tested and supported for PMML mode are "lm", "rpart", "glm", "multinom", "nnet" and "kmeans". You can type in any R code in the code editor of Open Source Integration node when you set the output mode to "Merge" or "None" in the parameter panel. In this paper, the PMML mode is used as it provides a strong integration for model management and automation.

There are some built-in macros in Open Source Integration node such as &EMR_MODEL, &EMR_CLASS_TARGET, &EMR_NUM_INPUT that make the coding in R easier for the data scientists. Instead of hardcoding the variable names, the metadata for the input variables can be managed by SAS nodes, which makes the modeling process more transparent and easier to follow.

A simple example for calling R Regression model (glm) in Open Source Integration node:

```
# Regression model
library(glm2)
library(pmml)
&EMR_MODEL <- glm(&EMR_CLASS_TARGET ~ &EMR_CLASS_INPUT + &EMR_NUM_INPUT,
data= &EMR_IMPORT_DATA, family= binomial())
```

A simple example for calling R Decision Tree model (rpart) in Open Source Integration node:

```
# Decision Tree model
library(rpart)
library(pmml)
&EMR_MODEL <- rpart(&EMR_CLASS_TARGET ~ &EMR_CLASS_INPUT + &EMR_NUM_INPUT,
data= &EMR_IMPORT_DATA, method = "class")
```

You can create Ensemble models by joining SAS and R models in SAS Enterprise Miner while searching for better accuracy. In the example below, SAS Decision Tree and R Regression models are joined in the Ensemble node:

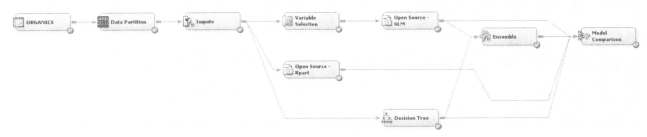

Figure 1. Developing R and SAS Models in SAS® Enterprise Miner™

As a result of the model build process with PMML, a DATA step score code is generated automatically, which is ready to be deployed in production.

A snippet of the generated code in the Open Source Integration node:

```
/*****************************************/;
*  PSCORE TIMESTAMP: 2017-23-1 19:3:27.43 ;
*  SAS VERSION: 9.04.01M4P110916 ;
*  SAS HOSTNAME: sasva ;
*  SAS ENCODING: wlatin1 ;
*  SAS USER: sasdemo ;
*  SAS LOCALE: EN_US ;
*  PMML Path: D:\opt\sasinside\SASWORK\_TD30744_SASVA_\emRPMML.xml ;
*  PMML SOURCE: Rattle/PMML;
*  PMML SOURCE VERSION: 1.4;
*  PMML TIMESTAMP: 2017-02-23 19:03:27 ;
*  MODEL TYPE: GeneralRegressionModel ;
*  MODEL FUNCTION NAME: Classification ;
/*****************************************/;

if missing("DemGender"n) then do;
    PSCR_WARN = 1;
end;
else do;
    "PSCR_AP0"n = "DemGender"n;
    if ( "PSCR_AP0"n not in ( 'F', 'M', 'U'  )  ) then do;

        PSCR_WARN = 1;
    end;
end;
...
```

The final step is the comparison of all models and selection of the champion to be deployed in production:

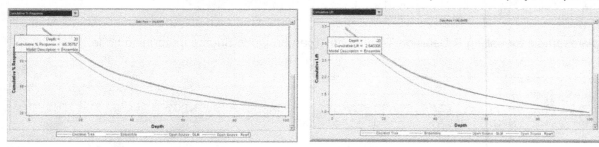

Figure 2. The Comparison of R and SAS Models in SAS® Enterprise Miner™

One of the reports generated by Model Comparison node is the Cumulative Captured Response chart shown on the left. It gives you the response rate for each decile ordered by the probability score. If you want to target top 20% of your customer base, you can explore the response rate for that percentile, which is around 65.4% in this example. The Lift chart on the right shows how better this response is compared to a random selection.

The results for the Ensemble model and SAS Decision Tree model are very close. You might set the Ensemble model as the champion to see how the automation will be handled for the combination of R and SAS model. And the SAS Decision Tree model can be set as the challenger in SAS Decision Manager.

The modeling process is now completed. In the next step, you will execute the key components in SAS Enterprise Miner to enable the lineage and automation for R and SAS models.

STEP 2. ONE-CLICK AUTOMATION AND LINEAGE

SAS automatically generates and stores a universally unique identifier (modelUUID) for all models including the R models. Using this Model ID, when you want to monitor the performance of your campaign and evaluate the impact of the analytical model on the response rate, you will be able to trace it back even in a very complex and large-scale marketing environment where you execute hundreds of models with different versions. This feature would also be beneficial for regulated industries like banking where you need to explain the reasons for your decisions.

You can export your model into SAS Decision Manager with one-click using the built-in SAS macros for model development and monitoring.

Figure 3. The Simple Flow Providing Model Lineage and Automation in SAS Enterprise Miner

The unique model ID is automatically extracted from SAS Metadata when you execute your score code in SAS.

If you run in-database scoring, you can create the model ID in your output table by including the following code in the *scoring editor* of the SAS Code node that is connected to the champion model:

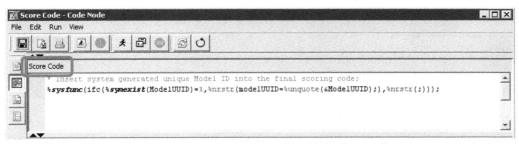

Figure 4. The SAS Code to Save the Unique Model ID for In-Database Scoring

The final node in the diagram above (One-Click to Manage) exports and registers your model into SAS Decision Manager.

The three parameters that will be used by %MM_Register macro are assigned at the beginning of the code in SAS Code node:

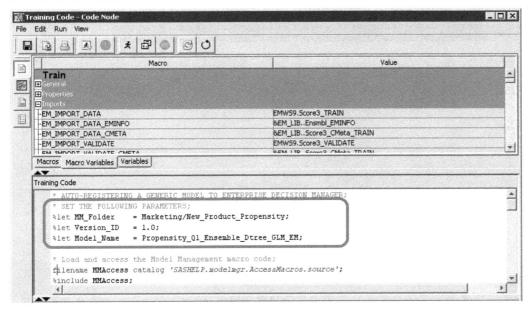

Figure 5. The One-Click Export SAS Code (Part-1) for Assigning the Parameters

The last part of the code in SAS Code node is a generic code that is parametric and can be used for exporting any model directly from SAS Enterprise Miner into SAS Decision Manager:

Figure 6. The One-Click Export SAS Code (Part 2) for Exporting and Registering

This champion model is now stored in SAS Decision Manager, ready to be published and monitored.

STEP 3. MONITOR PERFORMANCE OF OPEN SOURCE MODELS

SAS Decision Manager is the centralized management environment for all the models that could be developed within different departments of your organization.

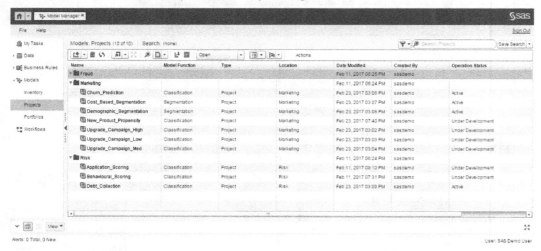

Figure 7. The Enterprise-Level Management of SAS and R Models in SAS

You can view the models that you exported to your &MM_Folder, which is set as a parameter in the SAS Code node in SAS Enterprise Miner. You can also import models from SPK files (SAS package) which enables the retraining functionality of R models in SAS Decision Manager:

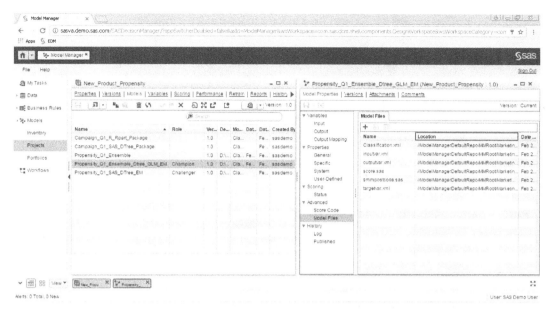

Figure 8. Auto-Registered R and SAS Models for New Product Propensity Analysis

You find the unique model ID (UUID) in the System tab of the model in SAS Decision Manager:

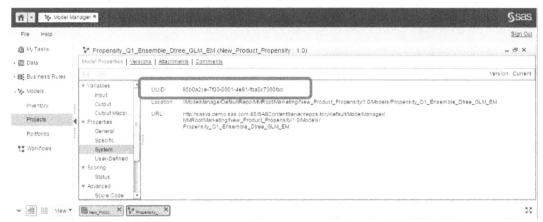

Figure 9. Unique Model ID Automatically Generated for the Ensemble Model

The same ID is generated in the output table when you execute the score code:

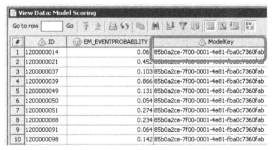

Figure 10. Unique Model ID Saved in the Score Dataset in SAS® Data Integration Studio

You can now build the monitoring jobs and start tracking the performance of R and SAS models. You can either use the GUI or MM macros to accomplish this task.

Monitoring the deviations in input characteristics and performance changes in time:

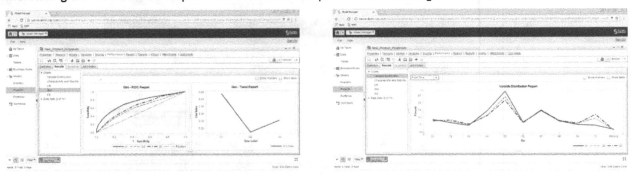

Figure 11. Model Performance Reports Generated for SAS® and R Models

There is a degradation in the performance of the Ensemble model when you look at the difference in Gini between the Q1 and Q3. SAS Decision Manager creates alerts when the models degenerate and sends notifications to pre-assigned users so that they can execute the retraining process or retire the model. The retraining can also be triggered automatically.

The next step will show the retraining of R models in SAS.

STEP 4. RETRAIN OPEN SOURCE MODELS

After importing the R model from SPK file, you define the retraining job in SAS Decision Manager and decide if the retrained model will be added to the existing version or to a new version.

Figure 12. Set up a Retrain Job for R Rpart Model

After the execution, the final list of SAS and R models in SAS Decision Manager are updated to include the retrained models which are automatically renamed with the time stamp:

Name	Role	Version
Campaign_Q1_R_Rpart_Package		1.0
Campaign_Q1_R_Rpart_Package_20170218T142806		1.0
Campaign_Q1_SAS_DTree_Package		1.0
Campaign_Q1_SAS_DTree_Package_20170218T141330		1.0
Propensity_Q1_Ensemble_Dtree_GLM_EM	Champion	1.0
Propensity_Q1_SAS_DTree_EM	Challenger	1.0

Figure 13. The List in SAS Decision Manager Including Retrained R and SAS Models

You can now compare the existing and retrained model and publish the one that performs better into production (in SAS or in-database) using the publish task in SAS Decision Manager or run the model in real-time.

In the next step, an example for an ad hoc analysis on model scores for Python developers is given.

STEP 5. AD HOC ANALYSIS OF PRODUCTION MODELS FROM PYTHON

You can download the module called SASPy from GitHub to connect to SAS 9.4 from Python. SASPy is a package that provides Python APIs to SAS and opens up all the data manipulation and analytical capabilities of your SAS System to the Python interface. It also supports the distributed computing. You can start a session and run SAS analytics from Python through the object-oriented methods. You can also use Jupyter magics which are available with the SASPy package and enable you to submit your SAS code to your SAS session from Python kernel. SASPy allows you to work in collaboration and utilize both SAS and Python skills for analytics.

In this example, you will see the usage of "sas_magic" to execute SAS code and Python together in Jupyter notebook.

```
# Load SAS magic from saspy package;
%load_ext saspy.sas_magic
%lsmagic

The saspy.sas_magic extension is already loaded. To reload it, use:
  %reload_ext saspy.sas_magic

Available line magics:
%alias  %alias_magic  %autocall  %automagic  %autosave  %bookmark  %cat  %cd  %clear  %colors  %config  %connect_info  %cp  %de
bug  %dhist  %dirs  %doctest_mode  %ed  %edit  %env  %gui  %hist  %history  %install_default_config  %install_ext  %install_pro
files  %killbgscripts  %ldir  %less  %lf  %lk  %ll  %load  %load_ext  %loadpy  %logoff  %logon  %logstart  %logstate  %logstop
%ls  %lsmagic  %lx  %macro  %magic  %man  %matplotlib  %mkdir  %more  %mv  %notebook  %page  %pastebin  %pdb  %pdef  %pdoc  %pf
ile  %pinfo  %pinfo2  %popd  %pprint  %precision  %profile  %prun  %psearch  %psource  %pushd  %pwd  %pycat  %pylab  %qtconsole
  %quickref  %recall  %rehashx  %reload_ext  %rep  %rerun  %reset  %reset_selective  %rm  %rmdir  %run  %save  %sc  %set_env  %
store  %sx  %system  %tb  %time  %timeit  %unalias  %unload_ext  %who  %who_ls  %whos  %xdel  %xmode

Available cell magics:
%%!  %%HTML  %%IML  %%OPTMODEL  %%SAS  %%SVG  %%bash  %%capture  %%debug  %%file  %%html  %%javascript  %%latex  %%perl  %%prun
%%pypy  %%python  %%python2  %%python3  %%ruby  %%script  %%sh  %%svg  %%sx  %%system  %%time  %%timeit  %%writefile

Automagic is ON, % prefix IS NOT needed for line magics.
```

Figure 15. Import SAS Package for Calling SAS® Code in Python from Jupyter Notebook

When you include %%SAS magic at the top of the cell in your Jupyter notebook, you can execute any SAS code within that cell. In the example below, you extract the list of all projects in the repository under the Marketing folder, which also includes "New_Product_Propensity" project.

```
%%SAS

%let projectModelsUrl = "http://sasva.demo.sas.com/SASContentServer/repository/default/ModelManager/MMRoot/Marketing";

filename output "/home/sasdemo/mm/models.txt";

proc http
    method="GET"
    out=output
    HTTP_TOKENAUTH
    url=&projectModelsUrl;
    headers
     ="Accept"="application/json";
run;

('<html><head><title>Jackrabbit 2.4.0 '
 '/default/ModelManager/MMRoot/Marketing</title></head><body><h2>default/ModelManager/MMRoot/Marketing</h2><ul><li><a '
 'href="..">..</a></li><li><a '
 'href="http://sasva.demo.sas.com/SASContentServer/repository/default/ModelManager/MMRoot/Marketing/Churn_Prediction/">Churn_Pr
ediction</a></li><li><a '
 'href="http://sasva.demo.sas.com/SASContentServer/repository/default/ModelManager/MMRoot/Marketing/New_Product_Propensity/">Ne
w_Product_Propensity</a></li><li><a '
 'href="http://sasva.demo.sas.com/SASContentServer/repository/default/ModelManager/MMRoot/Marketing/Upgrade_Campaign_Low/">Upgr
ade_Campaign_Low</a></li><li><a '
 'href="http://sasva.demo.sas.com/SASContentServer/repository/default/ModelManager/MMRoot/Marketing/Upgrade_Campaign_Med/">Upgr
ade_Campaign_Med</a></li><li><a '
 'href="http://sasva.demo.sas.com/SASContentServer/repository/default/ModelManager/MMRoot/Marketing/Cost_Based_Segmentation/">C
ost_Based_Segmentation</a></li><li><a '
 'href="http://sasva.demo.sas.com/SASContentServer/repository/default/ModelManager/MMRoot/Marketing/Upgrade_Campaign_High/">Upg
rade Campaign High</a></li><li><a '
```

Figure 16. The REST Call to Extract List of Analytical Projects in Marketing Repository

When you find the name of your project on that list, you can rerun the same code by updating the path in the "projectsModelsURL" until you extract the name of the full path for the score code.

You then import the score code on your local drive via the following REST call:

```
%%SAS

%let scoreCodeUrl = "http://sasva.demo.sas.com/SASContentServer/repository/default/ModelManager/MMRoot/Marketing/
                    New_Product_Propensity/1.0/Models/Propensity_Q1_Ensemble_Dtree_GLM_EM/score.sas";
filename output "/home/sasdemo/mm/score.sas";

proc http
    method="GET"
    out=output
    HTTP_TOKENAUTH
    url=&scoreCodeUrl;
run;
```

Figure 17. The REST Call to Extract the Score Code for a Specific Model

In the next step, you run an ad hoc analysis on your historical campaign data sets. You join data from different time periods and score all of them to run a seasonality analysis:

```
%%SAS

libname saslib "/home/sasdemo/data";

# Scoring datasets for ad-hoc analysis of weather impact on target and correlation between scores and inputs.
data scores_weather_impact_test;
    set saslib.campaign_Q1  saslib.campaign_Q2  saslib.campaign_Q3  saslib.campaign_Q4;
    by DATE;
    %include "/home/sasdemo/mm/score.sas";
run;
```

Figure 18. The SAS Code to Extract List of Analytical Projects in Marketing Repository

Using Python, you can experiment new data from web or other external sources to search for new correlations with campaign responses. As an example, you can extract the weather information from web and analyze the temperature impact on your target:

```
# Download the JSON data from OpenWeatherMap.org's API.
import json, requests, sys
location = "London"

url ='http://api.openweathermap.org/data/2.5/forecast/daily?q=%s&cnt=3' % (location)
response = requests.get(url)

# Store weather data in a Python variable.
weatherData = json.loads(response.text)

# Print weather descriptions.
w = weatherData['list']
print('Current weather in %s:' % (location))
print(w[0]['weather'][0]['main'], '-', w[0]['weather'][0]['description'])
print()
print('Tomorrow:')
print(w[1]['weather'][0]['main'], '-', w[1]['weather'][0]['description'])
print()
print('Day after tomorrow:')
print(w[2]['weather'][0]['main'], '-', w[2]['weather'][0]['description'])
```

Figure 19. The Python Code to Extract Weather Data

You might run further analysis to investigate your temperature-sensitive products, such as record players (might be preferred more in cold weather companied by wine) or bicycles (less tempting in rainy seasons) or dehumidifiers (more demand in summer when the laundry doesn't dry indoors) and so on.

As a Python coder, you can extract this information and run quick tests. If you decide that some of the new variables will add value to your production model, you can then automate the extraction process. The utilization of different tools and skills in the organization will bring flexibility that promotes collaboration and innovation which improves your analytical efficiency.

CONCLUSION

This paper provides examples to demonstrate the integration of open source analytics and SAS 9.4 using a marketing use case. SAS serves as the enterprise platform that enables and integrates different tools and skillsets within the organization including open source, provides a collaborative working environment and automates the analytical life cycle which would ultimately increase the value you get from analytics.

REFERENCES

SAS Communities Library for R Installation. Available https://communities.sas.com/t5/SAS-Communities-Library/The-Open-Source-Integration-node-installation-cheat-sheet/ta-p/223470.

SAS Institute Inc. 2016. SAS Institute white paper. "SAS in the Open Ecosystem." Available https://www.sas.com/content/dam/SAS/en_us/doc/whitepaper1/sas-in-open-ecosystem-108574.pdf.

SAS Institute Inc. 2017. *SAS Model Manager 14.2: Macro Reference.* Cary, NC: SAS Institute Inc. Available http://support.sas.com/documentation/cdl/en/mdlmgrmacro/69923/PDF/default/mdlmgrmacro.pdf.

SAS repository on GitHub with code snippets. Available https://github.com/sassoftware/enlighten-integration.

SAS repository on GitHub for Python interface module to the SAS System. Available https://github.com/sassoftware/saspy.

SAS repository on GitHub for SAS Kernel for Jupyter Notebook. Available https://github.com/sassoftware/sas_kernel.

ACKNOWLEDGMENTS

Thanks to Andrew Pease, Larry Orimoloye, Cristina Conti, Sascha Schubert and Douglas Liming for their contributions to this paper.

CONTACT INFORMATION

Your comments and questions are valued and encouraged. Contact the author at:

Tuba Islam
SAS Software Inc.
tuba.islam@sas.com
www.linkedin.com/in/tubaislam

SAS514-2017

Automated Hyperparameter Tuning for Effective Machine Learning

Patrick Koch, Brett Wujek, Oleg Golovidov, and Steven Gardner

SAS Institute Inc.

ABSTRACT

Machine learning predictive modeling algorithms are governed by "hyperparameters" that have no clear defaults agreeable to a wide range of applications. The *depth* of a decision tree, *number of trees* in a forest, *number of hidden layers* and *neurons in each layer* in a neural network, and *degree of regularization* to prevent overfitting are a few examples of quantities that must be prescribed for these algorithms. Not only do ideal settings for the hyperparameters dictate the performance of the training process, but more importantly they govern the quality of the resulting predictive models. Recent efforts to move from a manual or random adjustment of these parameters include rough grid search and intelligent numerical optimization strategies.

This paper presents an automatic tuning implementation that uses local search optimization for tuning hyperparameters of modeling algorithms in SAS® Visual Data Mining and Machine Learning. The AUTOTUNE statement in the TREESPLIT, FOREST, GRADBOOST, NNET, SVMACHINE, and FACTMAC procedures defines tunable parameters, default ranges, user overrides, and validation schemes to avoid overfitting. Given the inherent expense of training numerous candidate models, the paper addresses efficient distributed and parallel paradigms for training and tuning models on the SAS® Viya™ platform. It also presents sample tuning results that demonstrate improved model accuracy and offers recommendations for efficient and effective model tuning.

INTRODUCTION

Machine learning is a form of self-calibration of predictive models that are built from training data. Machine learning predictive modeling algorithms are commonly used to find hidden value in big data. Facilitating effective decision making requires the transformation of relevant data to high-quality descriptive and predictive models. The transformation presents several challenges however. For example, consider a neural network, as shown in Figure 1. Outputs are predicted by transforming a set of inputs through a series of hidden layers that are defined by activation functions linked with weights. Determining the activation functions and the weights to determine the best model configuration is a complex optimization problem.

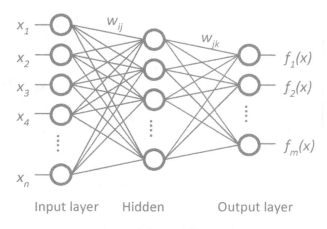

Figure 1. Neural Network

The goal in this model-training optimization problem is to find the weights that will minimize the error in model predictions based on the training data, validation data, specified model configuration (number of hidden layers and number of neurons in each hidden layer), and the level of regularization that is added to reduce overfitting to training data. One recently popular approach to solving for the weights in this optimization problem is through use of a *stochastic gradient descent* (SGD) algorithm (Bottou, Curtis, and Nocedal 2016). This algorithm is a variation of gradient descent in which instead of calculating the gradient of the loss over all observations to update the weights at each step, a "mini-batch" random sample of the observations is used to estimate loss, sampling without replacement until all observations have been used. The performance of this algorithm, as with all optimization algorithms, depends on a number of control parameters for which no default values are best for all problems. SGD parameters include the following control parameters (among others):

- a *learning rate* that controls the step size for selecting new weights

- a *momentum* parameter to avoid slow oscillations

- an *adaptive decay rate* and an *annealing rate* to adjust the learning rate for each weight and time

- a *mini-batch* size for sampling a subset of observations

The best values of the control parameters must be chosen very carefully. For example, the learning rate can be adjusted to reach a solution more quickly; however, if the value is too high, the solution diverges, and if it is too low, the performance is very slow, as shown in Figure 2(a). The momentum parameter dictates whether the algorithm tends to oscillate slowly in ravines where solutions lie (jumping back and forth across the ravine) or dives in quickly, as shown in Figure 2(b). But if momentum is too high, it could jump past the solution (Sutskever et al. 2013). Similar accuracy-versus-performance trade-offs are encountered with the other control parameters. The adaptive decay can be adjusted to improve accuracy, and the annealing rate is often necessary to avoid jumping past a solution. Ideally, the size of the mini-batch for distributed training is small enough to improve performance and large enough to produce accurate models. A communication frequency parameter can be used to adjust how often training information (such as average weights, velocity vectors, and annealing rates) is synced when training is distributed across a compute grid; higher frequency might increase accuracy, but it also reduces performance.

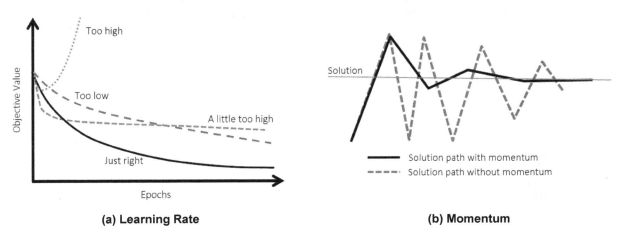

(a) Learning Rate   (b) Momentum

Figure 2. Effect of Hyperparameters on Neural Network Training Convergence

The best values of these parameters vary for different data sets, and they must be chosen before model training begins. These options dictate not only the performance of the training process, but more importantly, the quality of the resulting model. Because these parameters are external to the training process—that is, they are not the model parameters (weights in the neural network) being optimized during training—they are often called *hyperparameters*. Figure 3 depicts the distinction between *training* a model (solving for model parameters) and *tuning* a model (finding the best algorithm hyperparameter values). Settings for these hyperparameters can significantly influence the resulting accuracy of the predictive models, and there are no clear defaults that work well for different data sets. In addition to the optimization options already discussed for the SGD algorithm, the machine learning algorithms themselves have many hyperparameters. As in the neural network example, the *number of hidden layers*, the *number of neurons in each hidden layer*, the *distribution used for the initial weights*, and so on are all hyperparameters that are specified up front for model training, that govern the quality of the resulting model, and whose ideal values also vary widely with different data sets.

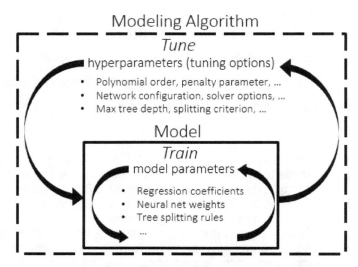

Figure 3. Model Training in Relation to Model Tuning

Tuning hyperparameter values is a critical aspect of the model training process and is considered a best practice for a successful machine learning application (Wujek, Hall, and Güneş 2016). The remainder of this paper describes some of the common traditional approaches to hyperparameter tuning and introduces a new hybrid approach in SAS Visual Data Mining and Machine Learning that takes advantage of the combination of the powerful machine learning algorithms, optimization routines, and distributed and parallel computing that running on the SAS Viya platform offers.

HYPERPARAMETER TUNING

The approach to finding the ideal values for hyperparameters (tuning a model to a particular data set) has traditionally been a manual effort. For guidance in setting these values, researchers often rely on their past experience using these machine learning algorithms to train models. However, even with expertise in machine learning algorithms and their hyperparameters, the best settings of these hyperparameters will change with different data; it is difficult to prescribe the hyperparameter values based on previous experience. The ability to explore alternative configurations in a more guided and automated manner is needed.

COMMON APPROACHES

Grid Search

A typical approach to exploring alternative model configurations is by using what is commonly known as a grid search. Each hyperparameter of interest is discretized into a desired set of values to be studied, and models are trained and assessed for all combinations of the values across all hyperparameters (that is, a "grid"). Although fairly simple and straightforward to carry out, a grid search is quite costly because expense grows exponentially with the number of hyperparameters and the number of discrete levels of each. Even with the inherent ability of a grid search to train and assess all candidate models in parallel (assuming an appropriate environment in which to do so), it must be quite coarse in order to be feasible, and thus it will often fail to identify an improved model configuration. **Figure 4**(a) illustrates hypothetical distributions of two hyperparameters (X_1 and X_2) with respect to a training objective and depicts the difficulty of finding a good combination with a coarse standard grid search.

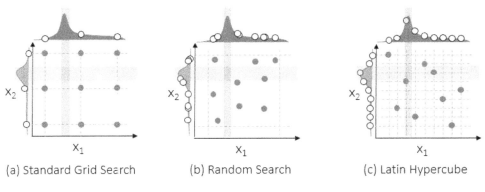

(a) Standard Grid Search   (b) Random Search   (c) Latin Hypercube

● = Individual model training and assessment

Figure 4. Common Approaches to Hyperparameter Tuning

Random Search

A simple yet surprisingly effective alternative to performing a grid search is to train and assess candidate models by using random combinations of hyperparameter values. As demonstrated in Bergstra and Bengio (2012), given the disparity in the sensitivity of model accuracy to different hyperparameters, a set of candidates that incorporates a larger number of trial values for each hyperparameter will have a much greater chance of finding effective values for each hyperparameter. Because some of the hyperparameters might actually have little to no effect on the model for certain data sets, it is prudent to avoid wasting the effort to evaluate all combinations, especially for higher-dimensional hyperparameter spaces. Rather than focusing on studying a full-factorial combination of all hyperparameter values, studying random combinations enables you to explore more values of each hyperparameter at the same cost (the number of candidate models that are trained and assessed). Figure 4(b) depicts a potential random distribution with the same budget of evaluations (nine points in this example) as shown for the grid search in Figure 4(a), highlighting the potential to find better hyperparameter values. Still, the effectiveness of evaluating purely random combinations of hyperparameter values is subject to the size and uniformity of the sample; candidate combinations can be concentrated in regions that completely omit the most effective values of one or more of the hyperparameters.

Latin Hypercube Sampling

A similar but more structured approach is to use a random Latin hypercube sample (LHS) (McKay 1992), an experimental design in which samples are exactly uniform across each hyperparameter but random in combinations. These so-called low-discrepancy point sets attempt to ensure that points are approximately equidistant from one another in order to fill the space efficiently. This sampling allows for coverage across the entire range of each hyperparameter and is more likely to find good values of each hyperparameter—as shown in Figure 4(c)—which can then be used to identify good combinations. Other experimental design procedures can also be quite effective at ensuring equal density sampling throughout the entire hyperparameter space, including optimal Latin hypercube sampling as proposed by Sacks et al. (1989).

Optimization

Exploring alternative model configurations by evaluating a discrete sample of hyperparameter combinations, whether randomly chosen or through a more structured experimental design approach, is certainly a fairly straightforward approach. However, true hyperparameter optimization should allow the use of logic and information from previously evaluated configurations to determine how to effectively search through the space. Discrete samples are unlikely to identify even a local accuracy peak or error valley in the hyperparameter space; searching between these discrete samples can uncover good combinations of hyperparameter values. The search is based on an objective of minimizing the model validation error, so each "evaluation" from the optimization algorithm's perspective is a full cycle of model training and validation. These methods are designed to make intelligent use of fewer evaluations and thus save on the overall computation time. Optimization algorithms that have been used for hyperparameter tuning include Broyden-Fletcher-Goldfarb-Shanno (BFGS) (Konen et al. 2011), covariance matrix adaptation evolution strategy (CMA-ES) (Konen et al. 2011), particle swarm (PS) (Renukadevi and Thangaraj 2014; Gomes et al. 2012), tabu search (TS) (Gomes et al. 2012), genetic algorithms (GA) (Lorena and de Carvalho 2008), and more recently surrogate-based Bayesian optimization (Denwancker et al. 2016).

However, because machine learning training and scoring algorithms are a complex black box to the tuning algorithm, they create a challenging class of optimization problems. **Figure 5** illustrates several of these challenges:

- Machine learning algorithms typically include not only continuous variables but also categorical and integer variables. These variables can lead to very discrete changes in the objective.

- In some cases, the hyperparameter space is discontinuous and the objective evaluation fails.

- The space can also be very noisy and nondeterministic (for example, when distributed data are moved around because of unexpected rebalancing).

- Objective evaluations can fail because a compute node fails, which can derail a search strategy.

- Often the space contains many flat regions where many configurations produce very similar models.

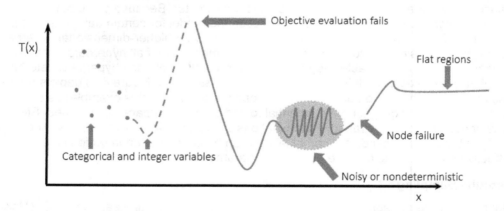

Figure 5. Challenges in Applying Optimization to Hyperparameter Tuning

An additional challenge is the unpredictable computation expense of training and validating predictive models using different hyperparameter values. For example, adding hidden layers and neurons to a neural network can significantly increase the training and validation time, resulting in widely ranging potential objective expense. Given the great promise of using intelligent optimization techniques coupled with the aforementioned challenges of applying these techniques for tuning machine learning hyperparameters, a very flexible and efficient search strategy is needed.

SAS Viya is a new platform that enables parallel/distributed computing of the powerful analytics that SAS provides. The new SAS Visual Data Mining and Machine Learning offering (Wexler, Haller, and Myneni 2017) provides a hyperparameter autotuning capability that is built on local search optimization in SAS® software. Optimization for hyperparameter tuning typically can very quickly reduce, by several percentage points, the model error that is produced by default settings of these hyperparameters. More advanced and extensive optimization, facilitated through parallel tuning to explore more configurations and refine hyperparameter values, can lead to further improvement. With increased dimensionality of the hyperparameter space (that is, as more hyperparameters require tuning), a manual tuning process becomes much more difficult and a much coarser grid search is required. An automated, parallelized search strategy can also benefit novice machine learning algorithm users.

LOCAL SEARCH OPTIMIZATION

SAS local search optimization (LSO) is a hybrid derivative-free optimization framework that operates in the SAS Viya parallel/distributed environment to overcome the challenges and expense of hyperparameter optimization. As shown in Figure 6, it consists of an extendable suite of search methods that are driven by a hybrid solver manager that controls concurrent execution of search methods. Objective evaluations (different model configurations in this case) are distributed across multiple evaluation worker nodes in a compute grid and coordinated in a feedback loop that supplies data from all concurrent running search methods. The strengths of this approach include handling of continuous, integer, and categorical variables; handling nonsmooth, discontinuous spaces; and ease of parallelizing the search strategy.

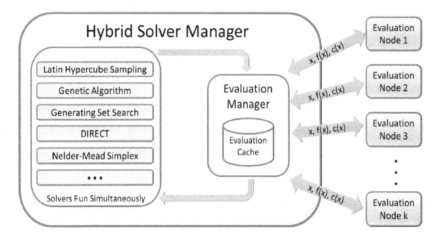

Figure 6. Local Search Optimization: Parallel Hybrid Derivative-Free Optimization Strategy

The autotuning capability in SAS Visual Data Mining and Machine Learning takes advantage of the LSO framework to provide a flexible and effective hybrid search strategy. It uses a default hybrid search strategy that begins with a Latin hypercube sample (LHS), which provides a more uniform sample of the hyperparameter space than a grid or random search provides. The best samples from the LHS are then used to seed a genetic algorithm (GA), which crosses and mutates the best samples in an iterative process to generate a new population of model configurations for each iteration. An important note here is that the LHS samples can be evaluated in parallel and the GA population at each iteration can be evaluated in parallel. Alternate search methods include a single Latin hypercube sample, a purely random sample, and an experimental Bayesian search method.

AUTOTUNING IN SAS MODELING PROCEDURES

The hybrid strategy for automatically tuning hyperparameters is used by a number of modeling procedures in SAS Visual Data Mining and Machine Learning. Any modeling procedure that supports autotuning provides an AUTOTUNE statement, which includes a number of options for specifically configuring what to tune and how to perform the tuning process. The following example shows how the simple addition of a single line (`autotune;`) to an existing GRADBOOST procedure script triggers the process of autotuning a gradient boosting model. The best found configuration of hyperparameters is reported as an ODS table, and the corresponding best model is saved in the specified data table (`mycaslib.mymodel`).

```
cas mysess;
libname mycaslib sasioca casref=mysess;

data mycaslib.dmagecr;
    set sampsio.dmagecr;
run;

proc gradboost data=mycaslib.dmagecr outmodel=mycaslib.mymodel;
    target good_bad / level=nominal;
    input checking duration history amount savings employed installp
        marital coapp resident property age other housing existcr job
        depends telephon foreign / level=interval;
    input purpose / level=nominal;
    autotune;
run;
```

Note: If your installation does not include the Sampsio library of examples, you will need to define it explicitly by running the following command:

```
libname sampsio '!sasroot/samples/samplesml';
```

After you run a modeling procedure that includes the AUTOTUNE statement, you will see (in addition to the standard ODS output that the procedure produces) the following additional ODS tables, which are produced by the autotuning algorithm:

- **Tuner Information** displays the tuner configuration.

- **Tuner Summary** summarizes tuner results, which include initial, best, and worst configuration; number of configurations; and tuning clock time and observed parallel speed up. (For more information, see the section "Autotuning Results and Recommendations.")

- **Tuner Task Timing** displays the time that was used for training, scoring, tuner overhead, and the overall CPU time that was required.

- **Best Configuration** provides the best configuration evaluation number, final hyperparameter values, and best configuration objective value.

- **Tuner Results** displays the initial configuration as Evaluation 0 on the first row of the table, followed by up to 10 best found configurations, sorted by their objective function value. This table enables you to compare the initial and best found configurations and potentially choose a simpler model that has nearly equivalent accuracy.

- **Tuner History** displays hyperparameter and objective values for all evaluated configurations.

Figure 7 shows some of the tables that result from running the preceding SAS script. Note that random seed generation and data distribution in SAS Viya will cause results to vary.

Tuner Information	
Model Type	Gradient Boosting Tree
Tuner Objective Function	Misclassification Error Percentage
Search Method	GA
Maximum Evaluations	50
Population Size	10
Maximum Iterations	5
Maximum Tuning Time in Seconds	36000
Validation Type	Single Partition
Validation Partition Fraction	0.3
Log Level	3
Seed	325840536

Tuner Summary	
Initial Configuration Objective Value	25.2492
Best Configuration Objective Value	22.9236
Worst Configuration Objective Value	32.6904
Initial Configuration Evaluation Time in Seconds	205.86
Best Configuration Evaluation Time in Seconds	199.53
Number of Improved Configurations	2
Number of Evaluated Configurations	45
Total Tuning Time in Seconds	1337.33
Parallel Tuning Speedup	4.7757

Tuner Task Timing		
Task	Seconds	Percent
Model Training	6294.43	98.55
Model Scoring	79.06	1.24
Total Objective Evaluations	6373.49	99.79
Tuner	13.25	0.21
Total CPU Time	6386.74	100.00

Best Configuration	
Evaluation	15
Number of Trees	121
Number of Variables to Try	18
Learning Rate	0.10852878
Sampling Rate	0.71321939
Lasso	2.36910431
Ridge	1.42146259
Misclassification Error Percentage	22.92

Tuner Results
Default and Best Configurations

Evaluation	Number of Trees	Number of Variables to Try	Learning Rate	Sampling Rate	Lasso	Ridge	Misclassification Error Percentage
0	100	20	0.100000	0.500000	0	0	25.25
15	121	18	0.108529	0.713219	2.369104	1.421463	22.92
39	120	18	0.117971	0.715619	2.518662	1.505052	23.92
10	76	18	0.450000	0.800000	7.777778	4.444444	24.25
44	122	17	0.167917	0.647899	2.607746	1.579147	24.25
37	125	18	0.101324	0.679376	2.287135	1.447222	24.58
38	124	18	0.087410	0.707852	2.034603	1.234505	24.58
14	71	20	0.088529	0.213219	0.755581	1.809792	24.92
30	122	18	0.099167	0.710840	2.220824	1.338587	24.92
1	100	20	0.100000	0.500000	0	0	25.25
6	121	9	1.000000	0.100000	4.444444	2.222222	25.25

Figure 7. SAS ODS Output Tables Produced by Autotuning

For each modeling procedure that supports autotuning, the autotuning process automatically tunes a specific subset of hyperparameters. For any hyperparameter being tuned, the procedure ignores any value that is explicitly specified in a statement other than the AUTOTUNE statement; instead the autotuning process dictates both an initial value and subsequent values for candidate model configurations, either using values or ranges that are specified in the AUTOTUNE statement or using internally prescribed defaults. Table 1 lists the hyperparameters that are tuned and their corresponding defaults for the various modeling procedures.

Hyperparameter	Initial Value		Lower Bound	Upper Bound
Decision Tree (PROC TREESPLIT)				
MAXDEPTH	10		1	19
NUMBIN	20		20	200
GROW	GAIN (nominal target)		GAIN, IGR, GINI, CHISQUARE, CHAID (nominal target)	
	VARIANCE (interval target)		VARIANCE, FTEST, CHAID (interval target)	
Forest (PROC FOREST)				
NTREES	100		20	150
VARS_TO_TRY	sqrt(# inputs)		1	# inputs
INBAGFRACTION	0.6		0.1	0.9
MAXDEPTH	20		1	29
Gradient Boosting Tree (PROC GRADBOOST)				
NTREES	100		20	150
VARS_TO_TRY	# inputs		1	# inputs
LEARNINGRATE	0.1		0.01	1.0
SAMPLINGRATE	0.5		0.1	1.0
LASSO	0.0		0.0	10.0
RIDGE	0.0		0.0	10.0
Neural Network (PROC NNET)				
NHIDDEN	0		0	5
NUNITS1,…,5	1		1	100
REGL1	0		0	10.0
REGL2	0		0	10.0
LEARNINGRATE*	1 E–3		1E–6	1 E–1
ANNEALINGRATE*	1 E–6		1E–13	1 E–2
*These hyperparameters apply only when the neural net training optimization algorithm is SGD.				
Support Vector Machine (PROC SVMACHINE)				
C	1.0		1E–10	100.0
DEGREE	1		1	3
Factorization Machine (PROC FACTMAC)				
NFACTORS	5			5, 10, 15, 20, 25, 30
MAXITER	30			10, 20, 30, …, 200
LEARNSTEP	1 E–3		1 E–6, 1 E–5, 1 E–4, 1 E–3, 1 E–2, 1 E–1, 1.0	

Table 1. Hyperparameters Driven by Autotuning in SAS Procedures

In addition to defining *what* to tune, you can set various options for *how* the tuning process should be carried out and when it should be terminated. The following example demonstrates how a few of these options can be added to the AUTOTUNE statement in the script shown earlier:

```
proc gradboost data=mycaslib.dmagecr outmodel=mycaslib.mymodel;
    target good_bad / level=nominal;
    input checking duration history amount savings employed installp
        marital coapp resident property age other housing existcr job
        depends telephon foreign / level=interval;
    input purpose / level=nominal;
    autotune popsize=5 maxiter=3 objective=ASE;
run;
```

Table 2 lists all the available AUTOTUNE options with their default values and allowed ranges. Descriptions of these options can be found in Appendix A.

Option	Default Value	Allowed Values
Optimization Algorithm Options		
MAXEVALS	50	[3–∞]
MAXITER	5	[1–∞]
MAXTIME	36,000	[1–∞]
POPSIZE	10	[2–∞]
SAMPLESIZE	50	[2–∞]
SEARCHMETHOD	GA	GA, LHS ,RANDOM, BAYESIAN
Validation Type Options		
FRACTION	0.3	[0.01–0.99]
KFOLD	5	[2–∞]
Objective Type Options		
OBJECTIVE	MSE (interval target)	MSE, ASE, RASE, MAE, RMAE, MSLE, RMSLE (interval target)
	MISC (nominal target)	MISC, ASE, RASE, MCE, MCLL, AUC, F1, F05, GINI, GAMMA, TAU (nominal target)
TARGETEVENT	First event found	
Tuning Parameters Options		
USEPARAMETERS	COMBINED	COMBINED, STANDARD, CUSTOM
TUNINGPARAMETERS	N/A	
Other Options		
EVALHISTORY	TABLE	TABLE, LOG, NONE, ALL
NPARALLEL	0	[0–∞]

Table 2. Autotuning Options

The following example shows how you can use the AUTOTUNE statement to specify several custom definitions of hyperparameters to be tuned. You can change the initial value and the range of any tuning parameter, or you can prescribe a list of specific values to be used by the autotuning process.

```
proc gradboost data=mycaslib.dmagecr outmodel=mycaslib.mymodel;
    target good_bad / level=nominal;
    input checking duration history amount savings employed installp
        marital coapp resident property age other housing existcr job
        depends telephon foreign / level=interval;
    input purpose / level=nominal;
    autotune popsize=5 maxiter=3 objective=ASE
        tuningparameters=(
            ntrees(lb=10 ub=50 init=10)
            vars_to_try(values=4 8 12 16 20 init=4)
        );
run;
```

In general, the syntax for specifying custom definitions of hyperparameters to tune is

TUNINGPARAMETERS=(*<suboption> <suboption> ...*)

where each *<suboption>* is specified as:

<hyperparameter name> (LB=*number* UB=*number* VALUES=*value-list* INIT=*number* EXCLUDE)

Descriptions of these options can be found in Appendix A.

PARALLEL EXECUTION ON THE SAS VIYA PLATFORM

Hyperparameter tuning is ideally suited for the SAS Viya distributed analytics platform. The training of a model by a machine learning algorithm can be computationally expensive. As the size of a training data set grows, not only does the expense increase, but the data (and thus the training process) must often be distributed among compute nodes because they exceed the capacity of a single computer. Also, the configurations to be considered during tuning are independent, making a sequential tuning process not only expensive but unnecessary, assuming you have an available grid of compute resources. If a cross-validation process is chosen for model validation during tuning (which is typically necessary for small data sets), the tuning process cost is multiplied by a factor of k (the number of approximately equal-sized subsets, called folds), making a sequential tuning process even more intractable and reducing the number of configurations that can be considered.

Not only are the algorithms in SAS Visual Data Mining and Machine Learning designed for distributed analysis, but the local search optimization framework is also designed to take advantage of the distributed analytics platform, allowing distributed and concurrent training and scoring of candidate model configurations. When it comes to distributed/parallel processing for hyperparameter tuning, the literature typically presents two separate modes: "data parallel" (distributed/parallel training) and "model parallel" (parallel tuning). Truly big data requires distribution of the data and the training process. The diagram in Figure 8(a) illustrates this process: multiple worker nodes are used for training and scoring each alternative model configuration, but the tuning process is a sequential loop, which might also include another inner sequential loop for the cross-validation case. Because larger data sets are more expensive to train and score, even with a distributed data and training/scoring process, this sequential tuning process can be very expensive and restrictive in the number of alternatives that can feasibly be considered in a particular period of time. The "model parallel" case is shown in Figure 8(b): multiple alternative configurations are generated and evaluated in parallel, each on a single worker node, significantly reducing the tuning time. However, the data must fit on a single worker node.

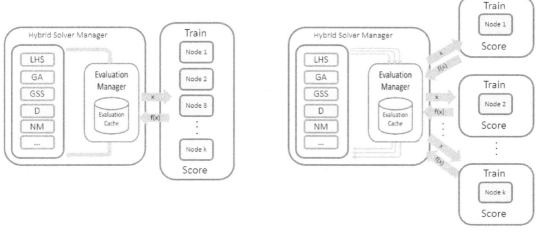

(a) "Data Parallel" (Sequential Tuning)   **(b)** "Model Parallel"

Figure 8. Different Uses of Distributed Computing Resources

The challenge is to determine the best usage of available worker nodes. Ideally the best usage is a combination of the "data parallel" and "model parallel" modes, finding a balance of benefit from each. Example usage of a cluster of worker nodes for model tuning presents behaviors that can guide determination of the right balance. With small problems, using multiple worker nodes for training and scoring can actually reduce performance, as shown in Figure 9(a), where a forest model is tuned for the popular **iris** data set (150 observations) for a series of different configurations. The communication cost required to coordinate distributed data and training results continually increases the tuning time—from 15 seconds on a single machine to nearly four minutes on 128 nodes. Obviously this tuning process would benefit more from parallel tuning than from distributed/parallel training.

For large data sets, benefit is observed from distributing the training process. However, the benefit of distribution and parallel processing does not continue to increase with an increasing number of worker nodes. At some point the cost of communication again outweighs the benefit of parallel processing for model training. Figure 9(b) shows that for a credit data set of 70,000 observations, the time for training and tuning increases beyond 16 nodes, to a point where 64 nodes is more costly than 1 worker node.

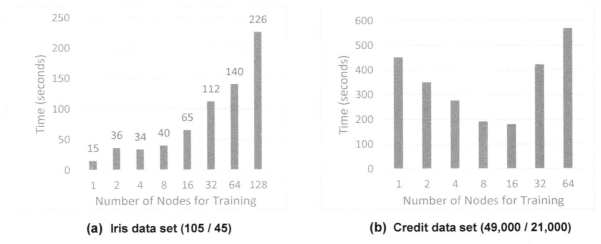

(a) Iris data set (105 / 45)   **(b)** Credit data set (49,000 / 21,000)

Figure 9. Distributed Training with Sequential Tuning for Different Size Data Sets (Training/Validation)

When it comes to model tuning, the "model parallel" mode (training different model configurations in parallel) typically leads to larger gains in performance, especially with small- to medium-sized data sets. The performance gain is nearly linear as the number of nodes increases because each trained model is independent during tuning—no communication is required between the different configurations being trained. The number of nodes that are used is limited based on the size of the compute grid and the search strategy (for example, the population size at each iteration of a genetic algorithm). However, it is also possible to use both "data parallel" and "model parallel" modes through careful management of the data, the training process, and the tuning process. Because managing all aspects of this process in a distributed/parallel environment is very complex, using both modes is typically not discussed in the literature or implemented in practice. However, it is implemented in the SAS Visual Data Mining and Machine Learning autotune process.

As illustrated in Figure 10(a), multiple alternate model configurations are submitted concurrently by the local search optimization framework running on the SAS Viya platform, and the individual model configurations are trained and scored on a subset of available worker nodes so that multiple nodes can be used to manage large training data and speed up the training process. Figure 10(b) shows the time reduction for tuning when this process is implemented and the number of parallel configurations is increased, with each configuration being trained on four worker nodes. The tuning time for a neural network model that is tuned to handwritten data is reduced from 11 hours to just over 1 hour when the number of parallel configurations being tuned is increased from 2 (which uses 8 worker nodes) to 32 (which uses 128 worker nodes).

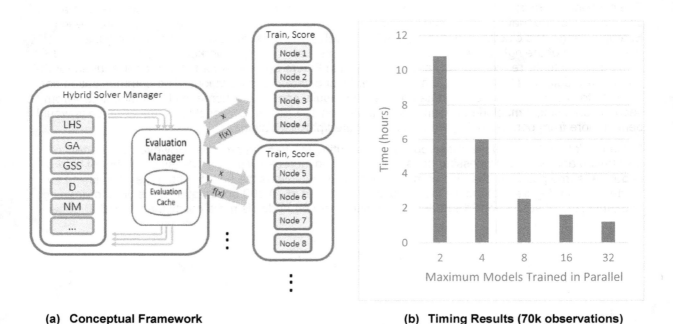

(a) **Conceptual Framework**   (b) **Timing Results (70k observations)**

Figure 10. Distributed/Parallel Training and Parallel Tuning Combined

AUTOTUNING RESULTS AND RECOMMENDATIONS

This section presents tuning results for a set of benchmark problems, showing that the tuner is behaving as expected—model error is reduced when compared to using default hyperparameter values. This section also shows tuning time results for the benchmark problems and compares validation by single partition of the data to cross-validation. Finally, a common use case is presented—the tuning of a model to recognize handwritten digits. Code samples that demonstrate the application of autotuning to these and other problems can be found at https://github.com/sassoftware/sas-viya-machine-learning/autotuning.

BENCHMARK RESULTS

Figure 11 shows model improvement (error reduction or accuracy increase—higher is better) for a suite of 10 common machine learning test problems.[1] For this benchmark study, all problems are tuned with a 30% single partition for error validation during tuning, and the conservative default autotuning process is used: five iterations with only 10 configurations per iteration in LHS and GA. All problems are run 10 times, and the results that are obtained with different validation partitions are averaged in order to better assess behavior.

Here all problems are binary classification, allowing tuning of decision trees (DT), forests (FOR), gradient boosting trees (GB), neural networks (NN), and support vector machines (SVM). Figure 11 indicates that the tuner is working—with an average reduction in model error of 2% to more than 8% across all data sets, depending on model type, when compared to a baseline model that is trained with default settings of each machine learning algorithm. You can also see a hint of the "no free lunch" theorem (Wolpert 1996) with respect to different machine learning models for different data sets; no one modeling algorithm produces the largest improvement for all problems. Some modeling algorithms show 15–20% benefit through tuning. However, note that the baseline is not shown here, only the improvement. The starting point (the initial model error) is different in each case. The largest improvement might not lead to the lowest final model error. The first problem, the **Banana** data set, suggests that NN and SVM produce the largest improvement. The **Thyroid** problem shows a very wide range of improvement for different modeling algorithms.

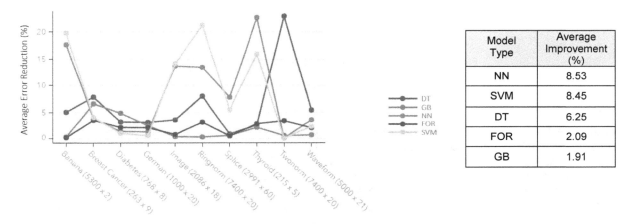

Model Type	Average Improvement (%)
NN	8.53
SVM	8.45
DT	6.25
FOR	2.09
GB	1.91

Figure 11. Benchmark Results: Average Improvement (Error Reduction) after Tuning

Figure 12 shows the final tuned model error—as averaged across the 10 tuning runs that use different validation partitions—for each problem and each modeling algorithm. The effect of the "no free lunch" theorem is quite evident here—different modeling algorithms are best for different problems. Consider the two data sets that were selected previously. For the **Banana** data set, you can see that although the improvement was best for NN and SVM, the final errors are highest for these two algorithms, indicating that the default models were worse for these modeling algorithms for this particular data set. All other modeling algorithms produce very similar error of around 10%—less than half the error from NN and SVM in this case. For the **Thyroid** data (which showed an even larger range of improvement for all modeling algorithms), the resulting model error is actually similar for different algorithms; again the default starting point is different, confirming the challenge of setting good defaults.

Overall, the benchmark results, when averaged across all data sets, are as expected. Decision trees are the simplest models and result in the highest overall average model error. If you build a forest of trees (a

---

[1] Data sets from http://mldata.org/repository/tags/data/IDA_Benchmark_Repository/, made available under the Public Domain Dedication and License v1.0, whose full text can be found at http://www.opendatacommons.org/licenses/pddl/1.0/ .

form of an ensemble model), you can reduce the error further, and for these data sets, the more complex gradient boosting training process leads to the lowest model error. The average errors for NN and SVM fall between the simple single decision tree and tree ensembles. Kernels other than linear or polynomial might be needed with SVM for these data sets, and neural networks might require more internal iterations or evaluation of more configurations, given the discrete combinations of hidden layers and units. *So why not always use gradient boosting?* Aside from fact that it might not be best for all data sets and the desire to use the simplest model that yields good predictions, there is a trade-off between resulting model accuracy and tuning time.

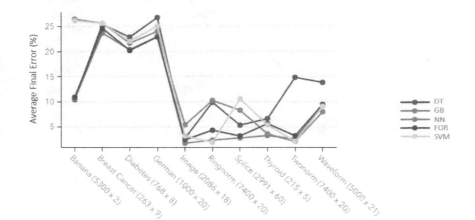

Model Type	Average Error After Tuning (%)
GB	9.9
FOR	10.7
SVM	13.1
NN	13.5
DT	13.9

Figure 12. Benchmark Results: Average Error after Tuning

TUNING TIME

For the tree-based algorithms, the trade-off is exactly the inverse ranking of machine learning algorithms with time compared to accuracy on average, as shown in Figure 13. Decision trees are the simplest and most efficient—only 14.4 seconds here for full tuning with this conservative tuning process. Building a forest of trees increases the time to over 23 seconds, and the complex gradient boosting process is more expensive at 30 seconds average tuning time. NN and SVM tuning times are similar for several problems, but higher for some, leading to a higher overall average tuning time; both use iterative optimization schemes internally to train models, and convergence might take longer for some data sets.

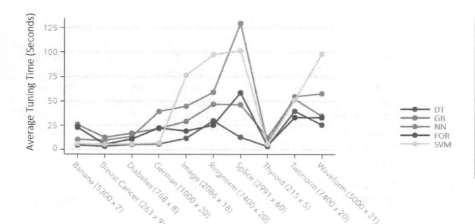

Model Type	Average Tuning Time (Seconds)	Average Parallel Speed-Up
DT	14.4	3.6
FOR	23.7	5.1
GB	30.0	4.7
NN	42.7	4.1
SVM	45.6	4.6

Figure 13. Benchmark Results: Average Total Tuning Time in Seconds

For these benchmark data sets, the tuning time is manageable—less than 30 seconds for fully tuning most models. Even the worst case, a neural network tuned to the wide **Splice** data set (which has 60 attributes) is tuned in just over two minutes. Note here again that all configurations are trained in parallel during each iteration of tuning. The total CPU time for this worst-case tuning is closer to eight minutes. With the default tuning process of 10 configurations during each of five iterations, one configuration is carried forward each iteration; so up to nine new configurations are evaluated in parallel at each iteration (by default). Figure 13 also shows parallel speed-up time (which is the total CPU time divided by the tuner clock time) of 3X–5X speed-up with parallel tuning. *Why is the speed-up not 9X with nine parallel evaluations?* Putting aside some overhead of managing parallel model training, the longest running configuration of the nine models that are trained in parallel determines the iteration time. For example, if eight configurations take 1 second each for training, and the ninth takes 2 seconds, a sequential training time of 10 seconds is reduced to 2 seconds, the longest-running model training. A 5X speed-up is observed rather than the average of the nine training times (1.1 seconds), which would be a 9X speed-up.

For larger data sets, longer-running training times, and an increased number of configurations at each iteration, the parallel speed-up will increase. For these benchmark problems, running in parallel on a compute grid might not be necessary; for a 30-second tuning time, 5X longer sequentially might not be a concern. Eight minutes for tuning the longer-running data sets might not even be a concern. Before you consider parallel/distributed training and tuning for larger data sets, however, you need to consider another tuning cost with respect to the validation process: cross-validation.

CROSS-VALIDATION

For small data sets, a single validation partition might leave insufficient data for validation in addition to training. Keeping the training and validation data representative can be a challenge. For this reason, cross-validation is typically recommended for model validation. With cross-validation, the data are partitioned into k approximately equal subsets called *folds*; training/scoring happens k times—training on all except the current holdout fold, and scoring on the holdout fold. The cross-validation error is then an average of the errors obtained from each validation fold.

This process can produce a better representation of error across the entire data set, because all observations are used for training and scoring. Figure 14 shows a comparison of cross-validation errors and the errors from a single partition, where both are compared to errors from a separate test set. The three smallest data sets are chosen, and the value in parentheses indicates the size of the holdout test set. Gradient boosting tree models are tuned in this case. The plot shows the absolute value of the error difference, where lower is better (validation error closer to test error). For the **Breast Cancer** data set, the single partition results and the cross-validation results are nearly equal. However, for the other two data sets, the cross-validation process that uses five folds produces a better representation of test error than the single validation partition does—in both cases, the cross-validation error is more than 5% closer to the test error.

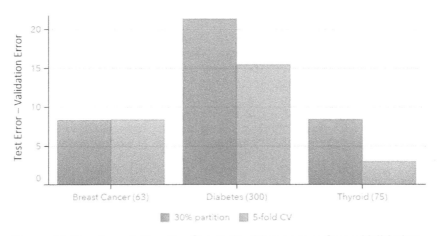

Figure 14. Benchmark Results: Single Partition versus Cross-Validation

With this cross-validation process, the trade-off is again increased time. The model training time, and therefore the overall tuning time, is increased by a factor of k. Thus, a 5X increase in time with sequential tuning for a small data set and a 5X increase with five-fold cross-validation becomes a 25X increase in tuning time. So tuning a model to even a small data set can benefit from parallel tuning.

TUNING MODELS FOR THE MNIST DIGITS DATA

In this section, the power of combined distributed modeling training and parallel tuning enabled by the SAS Viya distributed analytics platform is demonstrated by using the popular MNIST (Mixed National Institute of Standards and Technologies) database of handwritten digits (Lecun, Cortes, and Burges 2016). This database contains digitized representations of handwritten digits 0–9, in the form of a 28 × 28 image for a total of 784 pixels. Each digit image is an observation (row) in the data set, with a column for each pixel containing a grayscale value for that pixel. The database includes 60,000 observations for training, and a test set of 10,000 observations. Like many studies that use this data set, this example uses the test set for model validation during tuning.

The GRADBOOST procedure is applied to the digits database with autotuning according to the configuration that is specified in the following statements:

```
proc gradboost data=mycaslib.digits;
    partition rolevar=validvar(train='0' valid='1');
    input &inputnames;
    target label / level=nominal;
    autotune popsize=129 maxiter=20 maxevals=2560
             nparallel=32 maxtime=172800
             tuningparameters=(ntrees(ub=200));
run;
```

In this example, the training and test data sets have been combined, with the ROLEVAR= option specifying the variable that indicates which observations to use during training and which to use during scoring for validation. The PARTITION statement is used in conjunction with the AUTOTUNE statement to specify the validation approach—a single partition in this case, but using the ROLEVAR= option instead of a randomly selected percentage validation fraction. Because there are 784 potential inputs (pixels) and some of the pixels are blank for all observations, the list of input pixels that are not blank is preprocessed into the macro variable *&inputnames*, resulting in 719 inputs (see the code in Appendix B). For tuning, the number of configurations to try has been significantly increased from the default settings. Up to 20 iterations are requested, with a population size (number of configurations per iteration) of 129. Recall that one configuration is carried forward each iteration, so this specification results in up to 128 new configurations evaluated in each iteration.

A grid with 142 nodes is employed and configured to use four worker nodes per model training. *Why four instead of eight or 16 worker nodes per training as suggested in Figure 9?* There is a trade-off here for node assignment: training time versus tuning time. Using four worker nodes per training and tuning 32 models in parallel uses 128 worker nodes in total. If the number of worker nodes for training is doubled, the number of parallel models might need to be reduced in order to balance the load. Here it is decided that the gain from doubling the parallel tuning is larger than the reduced training time from doubling the number of worker nodes for each model training. Using four worker nodes, the training time for a default gradient boosting model is approximately 21.5 minutes. With eight worker nodes, the training time is approximately 13 minutes.

With up to 20 iterations and 128 configurations per iteration, the MAXEVALS= option is increased to 2,560 to accommodate these settings (the default for this option is 50, which would lead to termination before the first iteration finishes). The MAXTIME= option is also increased to support up to 48 hours of tuning time; many of the configurations train in less than the time required for the default model training.

Finally, the upper bound on the tuning range for the NTREES hyperparameter is increased to 200 from the default value of 150. The syntax enables you to override either or both of the hyperparameter bounds; in this example, the default lower bound for NTREES is unchanged and PROC GRADBOOST uses default settings for the other five tuning parameters. Increasing the upper bound for the *number of trees* hyperparameter will increase the training time for some models (and thus increase the tuning time) but might allow better models to be identified.

Some of the challenges of hyperparameter tuning discussed earlier can be seen in Figure 15, which shows the error for the configurations that are evaluated in the first iteration of tuning. Recall that the first iteration uses a Latin hypercube sample (which is more uniform than a pure random sample) to obtain an initial sample of the space. Two key points can be seen very clearly in this plot:

- The majority of the evaluated configurations produce a validation error larger than that of the default configuration, which is 2.57%.

- As you look across the plot, you can clearly see that many different configurations produce very similar error rates. These similar error rates indicate flat regions in the space, which are difficult for an optimizer to traverse and make it difficult for random configurations to identify an improved model.

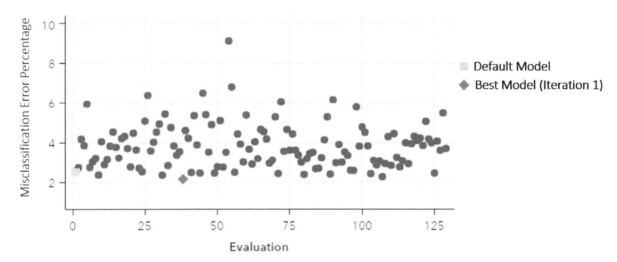

Figure 15. The GRADBOOST Procedure Tuning to MNIST Digits Data—Iteration 1

An improved model is found in the first iteration, with an error of 2.21%. Figure 16 shows the results of applying the genetic algorithm in subsequent iterations. The error is reduced again in 11 of the remaining 19 iterations. The tuning process is terminated when the maximum requested number of iterations is reached, after evaluating 2,555 unique model configurations. Here the final error is 1.74%. Details of the final model configuration are shown in Figure 17. The *number of trees* hyperparameter (which starts with a default of 100 trees) is driven up to 142 trees, still below the default upper bound of 150. Only 317 variables are used, well below the default of all (719) variables. *Learning rate* is increased from a default of 0.1 to 0.19, and *sampling rate* is increased from 0.5 to 1.0, its upper bound. Both lasso and ridge regularization begin at 0; *lasso* is increased to 0.14 and *ridge* is increased to 0.23.

Also shown in Figure 17 are tuning timing information and a tuning process summary. You can see that the tuning time of just over 28 hours (101,823 seconds) actually uses more than 760 hours of CPU time (the sum of all parallel training/scoring time for each objective evaluation), which results in a parallel speed-up of nearly 27X—much more than the 5X best case speed-up that is seen with the benchmark problems, and a much better ratio of 0.84 (with 32 parallel evaluations) compared to 0.56 (5X speed-up with 9 parallel evaluations).

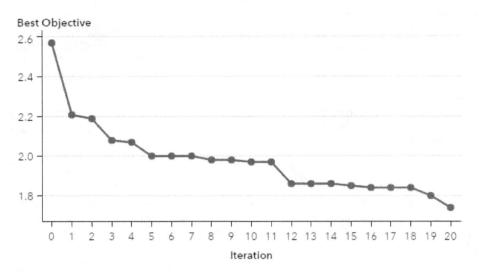

Figure 16. The GRADBOOST Procedure Tuning Iteration History, MNIST Digits Data

Best Configuration	
Evaluation	2551
Number of Trees	142
Number of Variables to Try	317
Learning Rate	0.19165378
Sampling Rate	1
Lasso	0.13883111
Ridge	0.2295815
Misclassification Error Percentage	1.74

Tuner Task Timing		
Task	Seconds	Percent
Model Training	2709131	98.98
Model Scoring	28018.86	1.02
Total Objective Evaluations	2737150	100.00
Tuner	26.84	0.00
Total CPU Time	2737177	100.00

Tuner Summary	
Initial Configuration Objective Value	2.5700
Best Configuration Objective Value	1.7400
Worst Configuration Objective Value	24.7200
Initial Configuration Evaluation Time in Seconds	1292.92
Best Configuration Evaluation Time in Seconds	1087.17
Number of Improved Configurations	18
Number of Evaluated Configurations	2555
Total Tuning Time in Seconds	101823
Parallel Tuning Speedup	26.8816

Figure 17. The GRADBOOST Procedure Tuning Results, MNIST Digits Data

CONCLUSION

The explosion of digital data is generating many opportunities for big data analytics, which in turn provides many opportunities for tuning predictive models to capitalize on the information contained in the data—to make better predictions that lead to better decisions. The tuning process often leads to hyperparameter settings that are better than the default values. But even when the default settings do work well, the hyperparameter tuning process provides a heuristic validation of these settings, giving you greater assurance that you have not overlooked a model configuration that has higher accuracy. This validation is of significant value itself.

The SAS Viya distributed analytics platform is ideally suited for tuning predictive models because many configurations often need to be evaluated. The TREESPLIT, FOREST, GRADBOOST, NNET, SVMACHINE, and FACTMAC procedures implement a fully automated tuning process that requires only the AUTOTUNE keyword to perform a conservative tuning process. This implementation includes the most commonly tuned parameters for each machine learning algorithm. You can adjust the ranges or list of values to try for these hyperparameters, exclude hyperparameters from the tuning process, and configure the tuning process itself. The local search optimization framework that is used for tuning is also ideally suited for use on the SAS Viya platform; alternate search methods can be applied and combined, with the framework managing concurrent execution and information sharing. With the complexity of the

19

model-fitting space, many search strategies are under investigation for both effective and efficient identification of good hyperparameter values. Bayesian optimization is currently popular for hyperparameter optimization, and an experimental algorithm is available in the local search optimization framework. However, the key feature of local search optimization is its ability to build hybrid strategies that combine the strengths of *multiple* methods; no one search method will be best for tuning for all data sets and all machine learning algorithms—there is "no free lunch."

The distributed execution capability provided by the SAS Viya platform is fully exploited in this autotuning implementation. With small data sets that might not require distributed training, the need for and added expense of cross-validation support the use of parallel tuning to balance the added expense. For large data sets, distributed/parallel training and parallel model tuning can be applied concurrently within the platform for maximum benefit. One challenge is selecting the right combination of the number of worker nodes per model training and the number of parallel model configurations. With small data sets, the number of workers per training should be set as low as possible and the number of parallel configurations as high as possible, allowing the compute grid nodes to be used for parallel *tuning*. With larger data sets, such as the MNIST digits data set, a balance must be struck. Usually hundreds of worker nodes are not needed for a single model training (even with truly big data) and there is always a communication cost that can be detrimental if too many nodes are used for training. With the number of configurations evaluated in parallel, there are never "too many"—the more configurations that are evaluated in parallel, the closer to 100% efficiency the tuning process becomes, *given that many parallel configurations are not all evaluated on the same worker nodes* (evaluating hundreds of configurations on four worker nodes simultaneously will slow the process down). Approximately 84% efficiency was achieved when the PROC GRADBOOST tuning process was used to model the MNIST digits data set.

What is not discussed and demonstrated in this paper is a comparison of the implemented hybrid strategy with a random search approach for hyperparameter tuning. Random search is popular for two main reasons: a) the hyperparameter space is often discrete, which does not affect random search, and b) random search is simple and all configurations could potentially be evaluated concurrently because they are all independent. The latter reason is a strong argument when a limited number of configurations is considered or a very large grid is available. In the case of the GRADBOOST procedure tuning a model to the MNIST digits data, four nodes per training and 32 parallel configurations uses 128 nodes. The best solution was identified at evaluation 2,551. These evaluations could not have all been performed in parallel. With a combination of discrete and continuous hyperparameters, the hybrid strategy that uses a combination of Latin hypercube sampling (LHS) and a genetic algorithm (GA) is powerful; this strategy exploits the benefits of a uniform search of the space and evolves the search using knowledge gained from previous configurations. The local search optimization framework also supports random, LHS, and Bayesian search methods.

With an ever-growing collection of powerful machine learning algorithms, all governed by hyperparameters that drive their fitness quality, the "no free lunch" theorem presents yet another challenge: deciding which machine learning algorithm to tune to a particular data set. This choice is an added layer of tuning and model selection that could be managed in a model tuning framework, with parallel tuning across multiple modeling algorithms in addition to multiple configurations. Combining models of different types adds a dimension of complexity to explore with tuning. With so many variations to consider in this process, careful management of the computation process is required.

You can specify the following options in the AUTOTUNE statement:

MAXEVALS=*number* specifies the maximum number of configuration evaluations allowed for the tuner.

MAXITER=*number* specifies the maximum number of iterations of the optimization tuner.

MAXTIME=*number* specifies the maximum time (in seconds) allowed for the tuner.

POPSIZE=*number* specifies the maximum number of configurations to evaluate in one iteration (population).

SAMPLESIZE=*number* specifies the total number of configurations to evaluate when SEARCHMETHOD=RANDOM or SEARCHMETHOD=LHS.

SEARCHMETHOD=*search-method-name* specifies the search method to be used by the tuner.

FRACTION=*number* specifies the fraction of all data to be used for validation.

KFOLD=*number* specifies the number of partition folds in the cross-validation process.

EVALHISTORY=*eval-history-option* specifies the location in which to report the complete evaluation (the ODS table only, the log only, both places, or not at all).

NPARALLEL=*number* specifies the number of configurations to be evaluated by the tuner simultaneously.

OBJECTIVE=*objective-option-name* specifies the measure of model error to be used by the tuner when it searches for the best configuration.

TARGETEVENT=*target-event-name* specifies the target event to be used by the ASSESS algorithm when it calculates the error metric (used only for nominal target parameters).

USEPARAMETERS=*use-parameter-option* specifies the set of parameters to tune, with *use-parameter-option* specified as:

STANDARD tunes using the default bounds and initial values for all parameters.

CUSTOM tunes only the parameters that are specified in the TUNINGPARAMETERS= option.

COMBINED tunes the parameters that are specified in the TUNINGPARAMETERS= option and uses default bounds and initial values to tune all other parameters.

TUNINGPARAMETERS=*(suboption . . . <suboption>)* specifies the hyperparameters to tune and which ranges to tune over, with *suboption* specified as:

NAME (LB=*number* UB=*number* VALUES=*value-list* INIT=*number* EXCLUDE), where

LB specifies a custom lower bound to override the default lower bound.

UB specifies a custom upper bound to override the default upper bound.

VALUES specifies a list of values to try for this hyperparameter

INIT specifies the value to use for training a baseline model.

EXCLUDE specifies that this hyperparameter should *not* be tuned; it will remain fixed at the value specified for the procedure (or default if none is specified).

```
proc cardinality data=mycas.digits outcard=mycas.digitscard;
run;

proc sql;
  select _varname_ into :inputnames separated by ' '
    from mycas.digitscard
    where _mean_ > 0
      and _varname_ contains "pixel"
    ;
quit;
```

REFERENCES

Bergstra, J., and Bengio, Y. (2012). "Random Search for Hyper-parameter Optimization." *Journal of Machine Learning Research* 13:281–305.

Bottou, L., Curtis, F. E., and Nocedal, J. (2016). "Optimization Methods for Large-Scale Machine Learning." arXiv:1606.04838 [stat.ML].

Dewancker, I., McCourt, M., Clark, S., Hayes, P., Johnson, A., and Ke, G. (2016). "A Stratified Analysis of Bayesian Optimization Methods." arXiv:1603.09441v1 [cs.LG].

Gomes, T. A. F., Prudêncio, R. B. C., Soares, C., Rossi, A. L. D., and Carvalho, A. (2012) "Combining Meta-learning and Search Techniques to Select Parameters for Support Vector Machines." *Neurocomputing* 75:3–13.

Konen, W., Koch, P., Flasch, O., Bartz-Beielstein, T., Friese, M., and Naujoks, B. (2011). "Tuned Data Mining: A Benchmark Study on Different Tuners." In *Proceedings of the 13th Annual Conference on Genetic and Evolutionary Computation* (GECCO-2011). New York: SIGEVO/ACM.

LeCun, Y., Cortes, C., and Burges, C. J. C. (2016). "The MNIST Database of Handwritten Digits." Accessed April 8, 2016. http://yann.lecun.com/exdb/mnist/.

Lorena, A. C., and de Carvalho, A. C. P. L. F. (2008). "Evolutionary Tuning of SVM Parameter Values in Multiclass Problems." *Neurocomputing* 71:3326–3334.

McKay, M. D. (1992). "Latin Hypercube Sampling as a Tool in Uncertainty Analysis of Computer Models." In *Proceedings of the 24th Conference on Winter Simulation* (WSC 1992), edited by J. J. Swain, D. Goldsman, R. C. Crain, and J. R. Wilson, 557–564. New York: ACM.

Renukadevi, N. T., and Thangaraj, P. (2014). "Performance Analysis of Optimization Techniques for Medical Image Retrieval." *Journal of Theoretical and Applied Information Technology* 59:390–399.

Sacks, J., Welch, W. J., Mitchell, T. J., and Wynn, H. P. (1989). "Design and Analysis of Computer Experiments." *Statistical Science* 4:409–423.

Sutskever, I., Martens, J., Dahl, G., and Hinton, G. E. (2013). "On the Importance of Initialization and Momentum in Deep Learning." In *Proceedings of the 30th International Conference on Machine Learning* (ICML-13), edited by S. Dasgupta and D. McAllester, 1139–1147. International Machine Learning Society.

Wexler, J., Haller, S., and Myneni, R. 2017. "An Overview of SAS Visual Data Mining and Machine Learning on SAS Viya." In *Proceedings of the SAS Global Forum 2017 Conference*. Cary, NC: SAS Institute Inc. Available at http://support.sas.com/resources/papers/ proceedings17/SAS1492-2017.pdf.

Wolpert, D. H. (1996). "The Lack of A Priori Distinctions between Learning Algorithms." *Neural Computation* 8:1341–1390.

Wujek, B., Hall, P., and Güneş, F. (2016). "Best Practices in Machine Learning Applications." In *Proceedings of the SAS Global Forum 2016 Conference*. Cary, NC: SAS Institute Inc. https://support.sas.com/resources/papers/proceedings16/SAS2360-2016.pdf.

ACKNOWLEDGMENTS

The authors would like to thank Joshua Griffin, Scott Pope, and Anne Baxter for their contributions to this paper.

RECOMMENDED READING

- *Getting Started with SAS Visual Data Mining and Machine Learning 8.1*
- *SAS Visual Data Mining and Machine Learning 8.1: Data Mining and Machine Learning Procedures*
- *SAS Visual Data Mining and Machine Learning 8.1: Statistical Procedures*

CONTACT INFORMATION

Your comments and questions are valued and encouraged. Contact the authors:

Patrick Koch	Brett Wujek	Oleg Golovidov	Steven Gardner
SAS Institute Inc.	SAS Institute Inc.	SAS Institute Inc.	SAS Institute Inc.
patrick.koch@sas.com	brett.wujek@sas.com	oleg.golovidov@sas.com	steven.gardner@sas.com

Random Forests with Approximate Bayesian Model Averaging

Tiny du Toit, North-West University, South Africa; André de Waal, SAS Institute Inc.

ABSTRACT

A random forest is an ensemble of decision trees that often produce more accurate results than a single decision tree. The predictions of the individual trees in the forest are averaged to produce a final prediction. The question now arises whether a better or more accurate final prediction cannot be obtained by a more intelligent use of the trees in the forest. In particular, in the way random forests are currently defined, every tree contributes the same fraction to the final result (e.g. if there are 50 trees, each tree contributes 1/50th to the final result). This ignores model uncertainty as less accurate trees are treated exactly like more accurate trees. Replacing averaging with Bayesian Model Averaging will give better trees the opportunity to contribute more to the final result which may lead to more accurate predictions. However, there are several complications to this approach that have to be resolved, such as the computation of a SBC value for a decision tree. Two novel approaches to solving this problem are presented and the results compared to that obtained with the standard random forest approach.

INTRODUCTION

Random forests (Breiman, 2001; Breiman, 2001b) occupies a leading position amongst ensemble models and have shown to be very successful in data mining and analytics competitions such as KDD Cup (Lichman, 2013) and Kaggle (2016). One of the reasons for its success is that each tree in the forest provides part of the solution which, in the aggregate, produces more accurate results than a single tree.

In the bagging and random forest approaches, multiple decision trees are generated and their predictions are combined into a single prediction. For random forests, the predictions of the individual trees are averaged to obtain a final prediction. All trees are treated equally and each tree makes exactly the same contribution to the final prediction. In this paper we question the supposition as model uncertainty is ignored.

Random forests are successful because the approach is based on the idea that the underlying trees should be different (if the trees were equal only one tree would be needed to represent the forest). This tree mixture is achieved by injecting randomness into the trees (this is explained in more detail in the following section). The resulting trees are diverse (by design) with varying levels of predictive power.

A goodness-of-fit statistic such as misclassification rate or average squared error may be used to judge the quality of each tree. Should the more predictive/accurate trees not carry more weight towards the final prediction? If the answer is affirmative, a second question needs to be answered: how should the trees be aggregated/amalgamated to get the best result?

In the rest of the paper a method of intelligent tree combination/aggregation, based on the theory of Bayesian Model Averaging, is proposed. Forests in SAS® Enterprise Miner is described in Section 2. The theory of Bayesian Model Averaging is explained in Section 3. For the theory of Bayesian Model Averaging to be applicable to decision trees, each tree's SBC value needs to be approximated. Neural networks are used to approximate the decision trees and this is explained in Section 4. A new weighting scheme is introduced in Section 5. Directly computing the degrees of freedom of a tree is reviewed in Section 6. The paper ends with a discussion and conclusions.

FORESTS IN SAS ENTERPRISE MINER

A random forest is an ensemble of decision trees. Multiple decision trees are constructed, each tree based on a random sample of observations from the training data set. The trees are then combined into a final model. For an interval target, the predictions of the individual trees in the forest are averaged. For a categorical target, the posterior probabilities are also averaged over the trees. A second step usually involves some kind of majority voting to predict the target category.

In SAS Enterprise Miner, the HPFOREST procedure (De Ville and Neville, 2013) takes a random sample (without replacement) of the observations in the training data set. This is done for each tree in the forest.

When each node in a tree is constructed, a subset of inputs is selected at random from the set of available inputs. Only the variable with the highest correlation with the target is then selected from this subset and used to split the node. Because many decision trees are grown, the expectation is that the better variables are more likely to be selected and that random errors introduced from overfitting will cancel when the predictions are averaged.

Our first attempt at Bayesian Model Averaging centered on the use of the HP Forest node in SAS Enterprise Miner (see Figure 1).

Figure 1. HP Forest node

However, because the node is "locked down", the user is unable to get access to the individual trees in the forest. Furthermore, the bagged sample (training data set) as well as the out-of-bag sample (testing data set) constructed by the HP Forest node are inaccessible. It is therefore impossible to use the output of one HP Forest node (in its current state) to implement our new approach. After some experimentation we decided on a different strategy.

The data set that is analyzed in this paper is the HMEQ data set. The data set contains 13 variables with loan default status (BAD) as the dependent variable and 12 independent variables, e.g. years at current job (YOJ), number of derogatory reports (Derogatories), number of delinquent trade lines (Delinquencies), etc. The data partition node was used to partition the raw data set into a training data set containing 80% of the data and a validation data set containing 20% of the data (see Figure 2). As the HMEQ data set is relatively small (only 5960 observations), and the training data set is again going to be divided into bagged and out-of-bag samples, the training data set was kept as large as possible without compromising the various model building steps that will follow.

Figure 2. Data partitioning of the raw data set

N different trees are constructed using N Decision Tree nodes. The trees are then aggregated as needed. But, the trees have to be different (as would have been the case if the HP Forest node was used). The solution is to use the HP Forest node for variable selection.

N HP Forest nodes (with different seeds) are used to construct N different forests, each containing a single tree. As each forest is built using different bagged (0.8) and out-of-bag samples (0.2), the trees in the forests should be very different from each other. Also to restrict the number of variables, the maximum depth of the trees in the forest has been set to three.

Although N trees (one from each forest) have been built, the details of the trees are hidden and access to the bagged and out-of-bag samples that were used to construct the trees are unavailable. But, information on the subsets of variables used to construct the forests (and therefore the trees) is accessible. These subsets are now used to construct N trees using Decision Tree nodes (see Figure 3). This strategy will force the N trees to be different.

Figure 3. HP Forest node used for variable selection

The HP Forest nodes are basically used as variable selection nodes so that the N decision trees that are constructed will be different from each other (simulating the strategy used by the HP Forest node). The trees will most probably not be exactly the same as that constructed by the HP Forest node (because the order of the splits are unknown and not all variables in the subset are available at each split), but the trees are built on the same subsets of variables used in the forests. The result is N different trees that can now be used to compare the different weighting schemes.

It might be tempting to use the N trees in the N forests to implement our new weighting scheme on. The problem is that each tree was built on a different bagged sample and also has an associated out-of-bag sample. Because the samples are not known, it is impossible to compute the goodness-of-fit statistics for the bagged or out-of-bag samples. The best that can be done is to consider the union of the different bagged and out-of-bag samples, which is the training data set.

As the HMEQ data set is small, partitioning the raw data set into three data sets to obtain a test data set is not practical (this would have been ideal to obtain an independent estimate of the performance of the models). The scoring data set therefore consists of the union of the training and the validation data sets, thus the raw hmeq data set (see Figure 4).

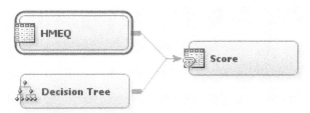

Figure 4. Scoring with a decision tree

This is a compromise and the fit statistics may therefore be optimistic. As only the relative performance of the models are important, all models are treated equally by scoring this data set.

The standard averaging implemented by the HP Forest node is now coded in a SAS Code node (see Figure 5) and the results computed on the scoring (hmeq) data set.

Figure 5. Computing goodness-of-fit measures

In this example, $N=5$ trees are constructed. Details of the number of leaves in each tree, the number of variables used in splitting and the depth of each tree are given in Table 1.

Tree	#Leaves	#Variables	Depth
1	10	3	5
2	5	2	4
3	16	4	6
4	14	4	6
5	16	4	6

Table 1. Five Trees

The c-statistic for the random forest based on these 5 trees is 88.3015, the misclassification rate is 14.89% and the sum of squared errors (sse) is 646.50. This is our *baseline* model and we will demonstrate in the following sections that a more intelligent amalgamation of the trees in the forest could result in a much better model with higher c-statistic, lower misclassification rate and smaller sum of squared errors (an indication of the variance of the errors).

BAYESIAN MODEL AVERAGING

When a single model is selected for predictive modeling, uncertainty about the structure of the model and the variables that must be included are ignored. This leads to uncertainty about the quantities of interest being underestimated (Madigan and Raftery, 1994). Regal and Hook (1991) and Miller (1984) showed in the contexts of regression and contingency tables that this underestimation can be large which can lead to decisions that have too high risk (Hodges, 1987).

In principle, the standard Bayesian formalism (Learner, 1978) provides a universal solution to all these difficulties. Let Δ be the quantity of interest, such as a future observation, a parameter or the utility of a course of action. Given data D, the posterior distribution of Δ is

$$pr(\Delta|D) = \sum_{k=1}^{K} pr(\Delta|M_k, D) pr(M_k|D) \quad (3.1).$$

The latter expression is the mean of the posterior distributions under each of the models, weighted by their posterior model probabilities. The models that are considered are $M_1, M_2, \dots, M_k$ and

$$pr(M_k|D) = \frac{pr(D|M_k) pr(M_k)}{\sum_{l=1}^{K} pr(D|M_l) pr(M_l)} \quad (3.2)$$

where

$$pr(D|M_k) = \int pr(D|\theta_k, M_k) pr(\theta_k|M_k) d\theta_k \quad (3.3)$$

is the marginal likelihood of model M_k, θ_k is the parameter vector of M_k, $pr(M_k)$ is the prior probability of M_k, $pr(D|\theta_k, M_k)$ is the likelihood, and $pr(\theta_k|M_k)$ is the prior distrubution of θ_k.

When averaging over all the models, a better predictive ability is obtained compared to using any single model M_j, as measured by a logarithmic scoring rule:

$$-E\left[\log\{\sum_{k=1}^{K} pr(\Delta|M_k, D) pr(M_k|D)\}\right] \leq -E\left[\log\{pr(\Delta|M_j, D)\}\right] \quad (j = 1, 2, \dots, K)$$

where Δ is the observable to be predicted and the expectation is with respect to

$$\sum_{k=1}^{K} pr(\Delta|M_k) pr(M_k|D).$$

This latter result follows from the nonnegativity of the Kullback-Leibler information divergence.

In practice, the Bayesian model averaging (BMA) approach in general has not been adapted due to a number of challenges involved (Hoeting, Madigan, Raftery and Volinsky, 1999). Firstly, the posterior model probabilities $pr(M_k|D)$ involve the very high dimensional integrals in (3.3) which typically do not exist in closed form. This makes the probabilities hard to compute. Secondly, as the number of models in the sum of (3.1) can be very large, exhaustive summation is rendered infeasible. Thirdly, as it is challenging, little attention has been given to the specification of $pr(M_k)$, the prior distribution over competing models. The problem of managing the summation in (3.1) for a large number of models has been investigated by a number of researchers. Hoeting (n.d.) discussed the historical developments of BMA, provided an additional description of the challenges of carrying out BMA, and considered solutions to these problems for a number of model classes. More recent research in this area are described by Hoeting (n.d).

Lee (1999) and Lee (2006) considered a number of methods for estimating the integral of (3.3) and came to the conclusion that the SBC may be the most reliable way of estimating this quantity. The SBC defined as

$$SBC_i = \log\left(\mathcal{L}(\hat{\theta}|y)\right) - K_i \log(n)$$

is used. In addition, a noninformative prior is exploited that puts equal mass on each model, i.e. $P(M_i) = P(M_j)$ for all i and j. The SBC approximation to (3.2) then becomes

$$pr(M_i|D) \approx \frac{P(D|M_i)}{\sum_j P(D|M_j)} \approx \frac{e^{SBC_i}}{\sum_j e^{SBC_j}} \quad (3.4).$$

The Bayesian approach automatically manages the balance between improving fit and not overfitting, as additional variables that do not sufficiently improve the fit will dilute the posterior, resulting in a lower posterior probability for the model. This approach is conceptually straightforward and has the advantage of being used simultaneously on both the problem of choosing a subset of explanatory variables, and the problem of choosing the architecture for the neural network (Du Toit, 2006).

When the SBC defined as

$$SBC_i = -2 \log\left(\mathcal{L}(\hat{\theta}|y)\right) + K_i \log(n)$$

is used, (3.4) becomes

$$pr(M_i|D) \approx \frac{P(D|M_i)}{\Sigma_j P(D|M_j)} \approx \frac{e^{-SBC_i}}{\Sigma_j e^{-SBC_j}}.$$

APPROXIMATING SBC WITH A NEURAL NETWORK

It is well-known that a decision tree can be used to approximate a neural network. This is usually done to gain some understanding of the neural network, as a neural network can be a black box. The converse, which is using a neural network to approximate a decision tree, is less obvious.

Just as with surrogate models (a surrogate model approximates an inscrutable model's predictions/decisions in order to facilitate interpretation), a neural network may be used to approximate the decision boundaries of the decision tree. As a neural network retains any non-linear relationships that are present in the decision tree, it is a good candidate for approximating a decision tree.

To apply the Bayesian Model Averaging formula of Section 3 to the trees in a forest, each tree's SBC is needed. This is not available as the degrees of freedom K for a decision tree is in general undefined. It is furthermore known that objective model selection criteria such as SBC cannot be used to compare models across different modeling techniques. It can only be used as a relative measure ranking models based on the same modeling technique. The expectation now is that the ranking of the decision trees from better to worse will be preserved in the SBC values computed by the neural networks.

Assume there are N decision trees in the forest. N neural networks are now constructed: each neural network approximating one tree. The number of hidden nodes in each neural network is adjusted to produce a neural network that closely shadows (in ROC curve and misclassification rate) the relevant tree (see Figure 6). As SBC is defined for neural networks in SAS Enterprise Miner, the neural network models' SBCs are now used as proxies for the decision trees' SBCs. Note also that SBC is only computed for the training data set by the Neural Network node, so this is what is used.

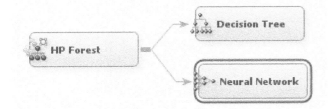

Figure 6. Approximating a decision tree with a neural network

The Neural Network node should be connected in parallel to the Decision Tree node and should have all the variables selected by the HP Forest node as inputs. If the Neural Network node is connected to the Decision Tree node, the Decision Tree node could do additional variable selection which may be undesirable. The training data set is used to construct the decision trees and the neural networks and the validation data set is used to optimize the decision trees as well as for stopped training in the neural networks.

Details of the $N=5$ constructed neural networks sorted by SBC are given in Table 2. All neural networks are multilayer perceptrons with one hidden layer and M hidden nodes.

Rank	Tree	# Hidden Nodes	SBC
1	2	4	3322
2	5	2	4032
3	3	4	4061
4	4	5	4393
5	1	5	4400

Table 2. MLP architectures

As the SBC values computed by the neural networks for the training data set used in this paper are large (3322 and greater), the base (e) used in the Bayesian Model Averaging formula, e.g.

$$\frac{e^{-3322}}{e^{-3322} + e^{-4032} + e^{-4061} + e^{-4393} + e^{-4400}}$$

creates computational difficulties and needs to be adjusted to make the computations viable.

When the base e is replaced by base 1, we get averaging:

$$\frac{1^{-3322}}{1^{-3322}+1^{-4032}+1^{-4061}+1^{-4393}+1^{-4400}} = \frac{1}{5}$$

as implemented in the HP Forest node in SAS Enterprise Miner (although SAS Enterprise Miner most definitely did not use the above formula to arrive at 1/5).

We therefore need a base greater than 1, but smaller than e to make the computations feasible. In this example, the base is adjusted to 1.002 (some experimentation might be needed to find and to adjust the base used in the formula so that reasonable weights are produced). The final weight computed for the best model is:

$$\frac{1.002^{-3322}}{1.002^{-3322} + 1.002^{-4032} + \cdots + 1.002^{-4400}} = 0.5867$$

Table 3 ranks the five models from good to bad giving their SBC values (smaller is better) as well as final weight contribution to the forest.

Rank	SBC	Weight
1	3322	0.5867
2	4032	0.1420
3	4061	0.1340
4	4393	0.0690
5	4400	0.0680

Table 3. Bayesian Model Averaging

The c-statistic for this model is 89.3474, the misclassification rate is 13.37% and the sse is 565.61. This gives an improvement of more than 1.18% in the c-statistic over the standard method used to construct the forest. The misclassification rate is reduced by 10.2% and the sse decreased by 12.5%. Because we do not have the degrees of freedom for the decision tree, we cannot compute the error variance (as is usually done for linear regression), but sse gives a good indication that the size of the errors decreased (the computed probabilities are more precise).

It is worth noting that the SBC is only used to weigh the contributions of each tree and that the underlying trees in the forest are not modified at all. The trees are only amalgamated in a more intelligent way using the computed weights.

A NEW WEIGHTING SCHEME

Approximating a decision tree with a neural network has its drawbacks: extra computation time is needed to train and adjust the neural network and the approximation may be imprecise. Finding the appropriate base to get a reasonable spread of the final weight might be an issue.

As we are only interested in the relative ordering of the models (from good to bad), sse or validation misclassification rate might also suffice. Table 4 lists the SBC and sse on the training data set for the neural networks as well as the sse on the training data set for the decision trees and the validation misclassification rate also for the decision trees.

Rank	TRAIN SBC NN	TRAIN SSE NN	TRAIN SSE DT	VALID MISC DT
1	3322	992	952	12.98
2	4032	1214	1168	15.74
3	4061	1185	1168	15.74
4	4393	1282	1280	16.41
5	4400	1296	1313	16.75

Table 4. SBC, SSE and MISC

Note how closely the neural network sse approximates the decision tree sse. Except for the tie in the 2nd and 3rd models, the decision tree misclassification rate on the validation data set mimics the ordering of SBC computed with the neural network. A simplification of the whole process is therefore to use the validation misclassification rate computed for each decision tree to rank the models.

But, the formula used to compute the final weights depends on SBC and this is now missing if we omit constructing the neural networks. The following weighting scheme can be used as an approximation to the formula of the previous section, and this only depends on the ordering of the models (as given in Table 4), not the absolute values of the computed SBCs.

If there are N trees in the forest, the weight for each tree i $(i = 1, 2, …, N)$ should be:

$$\left\{ \frac{2^{i-1}}{\sum_{k=0}^{n-1} 2^k} \right\}$$

For the hmeq data set with five trees in the forest, the weights are

$$\left\{ \frac{1}{31}, \frac{2}{31}, \frac{4}{31}, \frac{8}{31}, \frac{16}{31} \right\}$$

which seems reasonable and not that different from the weight computed with Bayesian Model Averaging. The table in the previous section is therefore updated to (see Table 5):

Rank	VALID MISC DT	Weight
1	12.98	0.5161
2	15.74	0.2580
3	15.74	0.1290
4	16.41	0.0645
5	16.75	0.0322

Table 5. Weights based on VALID MISC of DT

Note how closely these weights resemble the weights computed with SBC (see Table 2). The c-statistic for this model is 89.4178, the misclassification rate is 13.65% and the sse is 569.20. This gives a 1.12% improvement in the c-statistic, a 8.32% improvement in the misclassification rate and a 11.9% decrease in the sse.

Although not as good as the previous model, it is still a significant improvement over our baseline model. Furthermore, this is an extremely simple computation that would require very little time to compute.

The formula also generalizes to larger N as the contributions of the inferior models in the forest tend to approach 0. This makes intuitive sense as the effect of random errors are mitigated. If the misclassification rate on the validation data set is replaced with misclassification rate on the out-of-bag sample, it would be a simple step to update the HP Forest node with this new result.

APPROXIMATING THE DEGREES OF FREEDOM K

The problem when trying to compute SBC values for decision trees (highlighted in Section 2) is that we do not have the degrees of freedom K for a decision tree. The AIC and SBC information criteria considers the tradeoff between fit and complexity. The principle is to penalize the fit for the complexity. For a decision tree we need to count the number of independent parameters. In Ritschard and Zighed (2003)

$$K = (r - 1)(c - q)$$

is given as the degrees of freedom for a induced/constructed tree, where q is the number of leaves in the tree, r the number of variables in the tree and c the product of the number of distinct levels for each of the r variables in the tree.

Although the formula for K looks simple, for any tree of reasonable complexity with multiple occurrences of the same variable, and with continuous variables added, the formula became increasingly difficult to apply. K can also become extremely large for a seemingly simple tree.

However, this approach of directly computing K seems promising and will be further investigated in a follow-up paper.

DISCUSSION

The theory of Bayesian Model Averaging is well-developed and provides a coherent mechanism for accounting for model uncertainty. It is therefore surprising that it has not been applied directly to random forests.

Bayesian additive regression (Heranádez, 2016) was an attempt to create a Bayesian version of machine learning tree ensemble methods where decision trees are the base learners. BART-BMA attempted to solve some of the computational issues by incorporating Bayesian model averaging and a greedy search algorithm into a modelling algorithm.

The method proposed in this paper does not attempt to turn an ensemble of decision trees into a statistical model (with corresponding probability estimates and predictions). Furthermore, the base learners (e.g. decision trees) are only combined in a novel way to produce a more accurate final prediction.

The way the decision trees are combined depends on the ordering of the decision trees from more accurate to less accurate. This was first achieved by building a surrogate neural network model for each tree and using the neural network models' ordering as a proxy for the decision trees' ordering.

The improvement in c-statistic, misclassification rate and sse confirmed our supposition that there is a better way of combining trees than the standard averaging used in random forests. The improvement is summarized in Table 6.

Model	c-statistic	MISC Rate	sse
Random Forest (Ave)	88.30	14.89%	646.50
Random Forest (SBC)	89.34	13.37%	565.61
Random Forest (Scheme)	89.41	13.65%	569.20

Table 6. Results

The Bayesian Model Averaging on surrogate neural networks introduced in this paper elegantly mitigates the reliance on the expectation that random errors introduced from overfitting will cancel when the predictions are averaged. Complex models where overfitting might be an issue are penalized in their SBC values (because of the large degrees of freedom value K in the surrogate neural network) with a resulting reduction in weight or contribution to the final model. Smaller errors are introduced into the system than is the case with random forests and it pays off in a better final model with improved fit statistics.

A Bayesian approach for finding CART models was presented in Chipman, George and McCulloch (1998). The approach consists of two basic components: prior specification and stochastic search. The procedure is a sophisticated heuristic for finding good models, rather than a full Bayesian analysis.

In a sense the procedure outlined in this paper is also a sophisticated heuristic that is used to compute the contribution of each tree to the forest, but with full Bayesian Model Averaging implemented on surrogate neural networks instead of the actual decision trees.

CONCLUSIONS

Although only a small change was proposed to the random forest algorithm, the improvements as shown in this paper could be substantial. However, the method depends on computing SBC values for decision trees which is problematic as a decision tree is not regarded as a statistical model.

The way around this problem is to use the SBC computed by a surrogate neural network. This gave an ordering of the models from good to bad. This information was then used to vary the contribution of each decision tree to the final model. Although a smart approximation, it still required a neural network to be built.

In a further simplification, validation misclassification rate was used to rank models and the contribution of each model to the final prediction was computed with a novel weighting scheme. The last results were still substantially better than that of the standard random forest approach, but not as good as when a neural network was used to approximate SBC.

REFERENCES

Breiman, L. "Random Forests." Statistics Department, University of California Berkeley, CA. 2001. Available at http://leg.ufpr.br/lib/exe/fetch.php/wiki:internas:biblioteca:randomforest.pdf

Breiman, L. 2001b. "Random Forests." Machine Learning, Vol. 45(1):5-32.

Chipman, H. A., George, E. I. and McCulloch, R. E. 1998. "Bayesian CART model search (with discussion and rejoinder by the authors)." Journal of the American Statistical Association. Vol. 93:936-960.

De Ville, B. and Neville, P. 2013. "Decision Trees for Analytics Using SAS Enterprise Miner." SAS Press, Cary, USA.

Du Toit, J. V. 2006. "Automated Construction of Generalized Additive Neural Networks for Predictive Data Mining." PH.D. thesis. School for Computer, Statistical and Mathematical Sciences, North-West University, South Africa.

Heranádez, B. "Bayesian additive regression using Bayesian model averaging." 2016. Available at http://arxiv.org/abs/1507.00181

Hodges, J. S. 1987. "Uncertainty, policy analysis and statistics." Statistical Science, Vol. 2(3):259-275.

Hoeting, J. A. "Methodology for Bayesian model averaging: an update." Colorado State University. n. d. Available at http://www.stat.colostate.edu/~nsu/starmap/jab.ibcbma.pdf

Hoeting, J. A., Madigan, D., Raftery, A. E. and Volinsky, C. T. 1999. "Bayesian model averaging: a tutorial." Statistical Science, Vol. 14(4):382-417.

Kaggle. 2016. Available at https://www.kaggle.com/

Learner, E. E. 1978. "Specification searches: ad hoc inference with nonexperimental data." Wiley Series in Probability and Mathematical Statistics, John Wiley and Sons, New York.

Lee, H. K. H. 1999. "Model selection and model averaging for neural networks." PH.D. thesis. Department of Statistics, Carnegie Mellon University.

Lee, H. K. H. "Model selection for neural network classification." 2006. Available at http://citeseer.ist.psu.edu/leeoomodel.html

Lichman, M. "Machine Learning Repository." University of California, Irvine, School of Information and Computer Sciences. 2013. Available at http://archive.ics.uci.edu/ml

Madigan, D. and Raftery, A. E. 1994. "Model selection and accounting for model uncertainty in graphical models using occam's window." Journal of the American Statistical Association, Vol. 89(428):1535-1546.

Miller, A. J. 1984. "Selection of subsets of regression variables." Journal of the Royal Statistical Society, Series A, Vol. 147(3):389-425.

Regal, R. R. and Hook, E. B. 1991. "The effects of model selection on confidence intervals for the size of a closed population." Statistics in Medicine, Vol. 10:717-721.

Ritschard, G. and Zighed, D. A. 2003. "Goodness-of-fit measures for induction trees." Foundations of Intelligent Systems, Lecture Notes in Computer Science, Springer-Verlag, Berlin, Vol. 27:57-64.

ACKNOWLEGDEMENTS

The authors wish to thank SAS Institute for providing them with Base SAS and SAS Enterprise Miner software used in computing all the results presented in this paper. This work forms part of the research done at the North-West University within the TELKOM CoE research program, funded by TELKOM, GRINTEK TELECOM and THRIP.

CONTACT INFORMATION

Your comments and questions are valued and encouraged. Contact the author at:

Tiny du Toit
Tiny.DuToit@nwu.ac.za

Methods of Multinomial Classification Using Support Vector Machines

Ralph Abbey, Taiping He, and Tao Wang, SAS® Institute Inc.

ABSTRACT

Many practitioners of machine learning are familiar with support vector machines (SVMs) for solving binary classification problems. Two established methods of using SVMs in multinomial classification are the one-versus-all approach and the one-versus-one approach. This paper describes how to use SAS® software to implement these two methods of multinomial classification, with emphasis on both training the model and scoring new data. A variety of data sets are used to illustrate the pros and cons of each method.

INTRODUCTION

The support vector machine (SVM) algorithm is a popular binary classification technique used in the fields of machine learning, data mining, and predictive analytics. Since the introduction of the SVM algorithm in 1995 (Cortes and Vapnik 1995), researchers and practitioners in these fields have shown significant interest in using and improving SVMs.

Support vector machines are supervised learning models that provide a mapping between the feature space and the target labels. The aim of supervised learning is to determine how to classify new or previously unseen data by using labeled training data. Specifically, SVMs are used to solve binary classification problems, in which the target has only one of two possible classes.

The SVM algorithm builds a binary classifier by solving a convex optimization problem during model training. The optimization problem is to find the flat surface (hyperplane) that maximizes the margin between the two classes of the target. SVMs are also known as maximum-margin classifiers, and the training data near the hyperplane are called the support vectors. Thus, the result of training is the support vectors and the weights that are given to them. When new data are to be scored, the support vectors and their weights are used in combination with the new data to assign the new data to one of the two classes.

Many real-world classification problems have more than two target classes. There are several methods in the literature (Hsu and Lin 2002), such as the one-versus-all and one-versus-one methods, that extend the SVM binary classifier to solve multinomial classification problems.

This paper shows how you can use the HPSVM procedure from SAS® Enterprise Miner™ to implement both training and scoring of these multinomial classification extensions to the traditional SVM algorithm. It also demonstrates these implementations on several data sets to illustrate the benefits of these methods.

The paper has three main sections: training, scoring, and experiments, followed by the conclusions. The training section describes how to set up the multinomial SVM training schema. The scoring section discusses how to score new data after you have trained a multinomial SVM. The experiments section illustrates some examples by using real-world data. Finally, the appendices present the SAS macro code that is used to run the experiments.

SUPPORT VECTOR MACHINE TRAINING

Support vector machines (SVMs) are a binary classifier that seeks to find the flat surface (a straight line in two dimensions) that separates the two levels of the target. Figure 1 shows an example of a binary classification problem and the SVM decision surface. In this example, the support vectors consist of the two triangular observations that touch one of the dotted lines and the one hexagonal observation that touches the other dotted line. The dotted lines represent the margin, which indicates the maximum separation between the two classes in the data set.

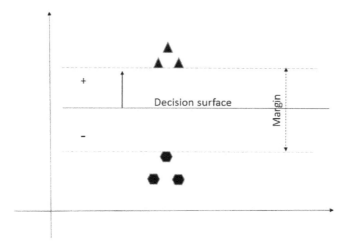

Figure 1. Support Vector Machine Decision Surface and Margin

SVMs also support decision surfaces that are not hyperplanes by using a method called the kernel trick. For the purposes of the examples in this section and the "Support Vector Machine Scoring" section, this paper is limited to referencing only linear SVM models. These sections equally apply to nonlinear SVMs as well. Figure 2 shows an example of two classes that are separated by a nonlinear SVM decision boundary.

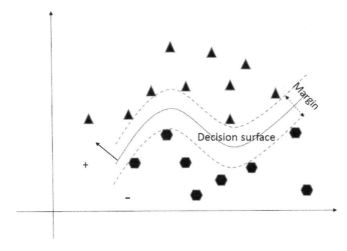

Figure 2. Nonlinear Support Vector Machine Decision Surface and Margin

Multiclass SVMs are used to find the separation when the target has more than two classes. Figure 3 shows an example of a three-class classification problem. Here the classes are triangle, diamond, and hexagon.

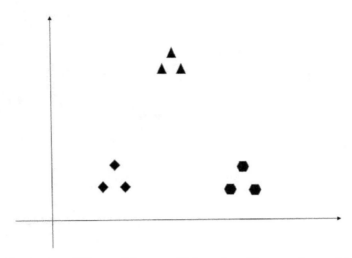

Figure 3. Example of Three Classes: Triangles, Diamonds, and Hexagons

When the data contain more than two classes, a single flat surface cannot separate each group from the others. However, several surfaces can partition the observations from each other. How you find the surfaces depends on your approach in the multiclass SVM: one-versus-all or one-versus-one.

When you are using the HPSVM procedure to solve multinomial classification problems, you first need to create a dummy variable for each class of the target variable. The dummy variable for a particular class is defined to be either 0 when an observation is not of that class or 1 when an observation is of that class. Code to create the dummy variables is presented in the SAS_SVM_ONE_VS_ALL_TRAIN and SAS_SVM_ONE_VS_ONE_TRAIN macros in Appendix B. An example that uses the data in Figure 3 might look something like this:

```
data ModifiedInput;
set Input;
   if (class = "Triangle") then do;
      class_triangle = 1;
   end;
   else do;
      class_triangle = 0;
   end;
   if (class = "Diamond") then do;
      class_diamond = 1;
   end;
   else do;
      class_diamond = 0;
   end;
   if (class = "Hexagon") then do;
      class_hexagon = 1;
   end;
   else do;
      class_hexagon = 0;
   end;
run;
```

When the input data have the dummy variables, the data are ready for you to train using the one-versus-all or one-versus-one method.

One-versus-All Training

The one-versus-all approach to multiclass SVMs is to train k unique SVMs, where you have k classes of the target. Figure 4, Figure 5, and Figure 6 show the three one-versus-all scenarios for training a multiclass SVM on the example from Figure 3.

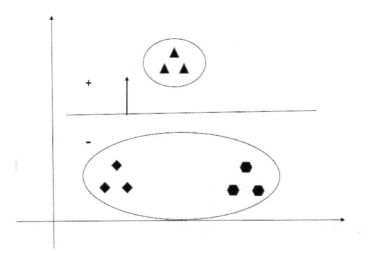

Figure 4. One-versus-All Training: Triangles versus All

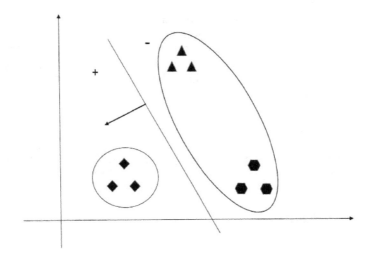

Figure 5. One-versus-All Training: Diamonds versus All

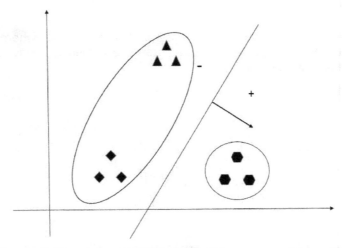

Figure 6. One-versus-All Training: Hexagons versus All

To set up the one-versus-all training by using the HPSVM procedure, you first need to add dummy variables to the input data set, as described previously. The dummy variable that corresponds to Figure 4 has a 1 for each triangular observation and a 0 for each diamond-shaped or hexagonal observation. The HPSVM procedure code for Figure 4 might look like this:

```
proc hpsvm data=ModifiedInput(where=(class=triangle OR class=hexagon));
   input <input variables>;
   target class_triangle;
run;
```

You also need to save the procedure score code by using the CODE statement. This enables you to score new observations based on the training that you have already completed. For the one-versus-all method of multinomial SVM training, you need to run the HPSVM procedure k times, and each run will have a different dummy variable as the target variable for the SVM. The output that you need for scoring is k different DATA step score code files. You can find a discussion of scoring the one-versus-all method in the section "One-versus-All Scoring."

One-versus-One Training

The one-versus-one approach to multiclass SVMs is to train an SVM for each pair of target classes. When you have k classes, the number of SVMs to be trained is $k*(k-1)/2$. Figure 7, Figure 8, and Figure 9 show the three one-versus-one scenarios for training a multiclass SVM on the example from Figure 3.

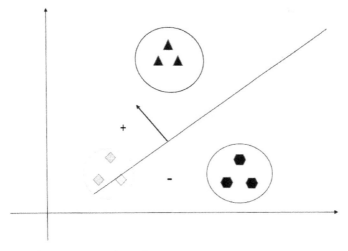

Figure 7. One-versus-One Training: Triangles versus Hexagons

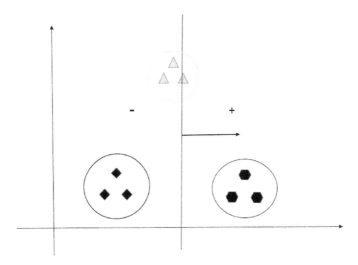

Figure 8. One-versus-One Training: Hexagons versus Diamonds

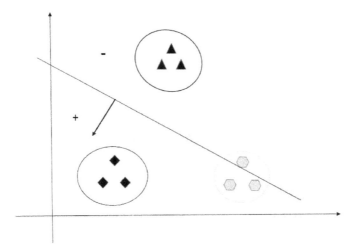

Figure 9. One-versus-One Training: Diamonds versus Triangles

As these three figures show, when you are using the one-versus-one training method of multinomial classification, you ignore any of the data that are not in the current comparison. For this example, you have three comparisons: triangular versus hexagonal observations, hexagonal versus diamond-shaped observations, and diamond-shaped versus triangular observations. In each of these cases, the third class is ignored when you create the SVM model.

To perform this method by using the HPSVM procedure, you first need to create the dummy variables as previously indicated. To ensure that you compare only the proper observations, you also need to subset the input data by using the WHERE= option. An example of the code for triangular versus hexagonal observations might look like this:

```
proc hpsvm data=ModifiedInput(where=(class=triangle OR class=hexagon);
   input <input variables>;
   target class_triangle;
run;
```

As in the one-versus-all method, you need to save the procedure score code by using the CODE statement. This enables you to score new observations based on the training that you have already completed. For the one-versus-one method of multinomial SVM training, you need to run PROC HPSVM $k*(k–1)/2$ times. Each run consists of a different pair of target classes that are compared. The output that you need for scoring is $k*(k–1)/2$ different DATA step score code files. There are two ways to score the one-versus-one training; they are detailed in the sections "One-versus-One Scoring" and "Directed Acyclic Graph Scoring."

SUPPORT VECTOR MACHINE SCORING

Scoring by using SVMs is the process of using a trained model to assign a class label to a new observation. In the case of the HPSVM procedure, the DATA step score code contains the information from the SVM model and enables you to score new observations. A new example observation, star, has been added to the previous example to illustrate scoring. This is shown in Figure 10.

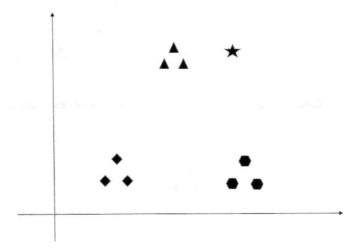

Figure 10. Example Data, with a New Observation (Star) to Be Scored

One-versus-All Scoring

The output from the one-versus-all scoring is k DATA step score code files, one for each class of the multinomial target. When you are determining the class of a new data observation, you need to score the observation by using each saved score code.

To assign a class label to a new observation, you need to score the observation scored according to each SVM model. In this way, the new observation will have an assigned probability for each class of the target. If the observation is on the negative side of the dividing hyperplane, then its probability is less than 0.5. If it is on the positive side of the dividing hyperplane, then its probability is greater than 0.5.

In this example, the hyperplanes shown in Figure 4, Figure 5, and Figure 6 illustrate that the star point will have the highest probability of assignment to the triangular class.

When you are using the PROC HPSVM score code for each class of the target, new data are assigned a probability that the observation is of that target class. To determine which target class is the correct label, you choose the one that has the highest probability. SAS macro code to do this is presented in the SAS_SVM_ONE_VS_ALL_SCORING macro in Appendix B.

One-versus-One Scoring

The output from one-versus-one scoring is $k*(k-1)/2$ DATA step score code files, one for each pairwise comparison of target classes of the multinomial target. When you are determining the class label of a new data observation, you need to score the observation by using each saved score code.

In one-versus-all scoring, each SVM model answers the question, Does this belong to the class or not? In one-versus-one scoring, each SVM model answers a different question: Is this more of class A or class B? Thus, using the maximum probability, as in one-versus-all scoring, is not the appropriate way to determine the class label assignment.

In one-versus-one scoring, a common method of determining this assignment is by voting. Each observation is assigned a class label for each SVM model that is produced. The label that the observation is assigned the most is considered the true label.

When you are using PROC HPSVM, use the score code to score the new data for each one-versus-one SVM model. Then, for each class of the multinomial target, check to see whether that class has the most votes. If it does, then assign that class as the label for the target. When you have a tie, you can assign the class randomly, or as shown in this paper, you can assign the class by using the first class in the sorted order. SAS macro code to perform one-versus-one scoring is presented in the SAS_SVM_ONE_VS_ONE_SCORING macro in Appendix B.

Directed Acyclic Graph Scoring

The directed acyclic graph (DAG), which was first presented in Platt, Cristianini, and Shawe-Taylor (2000), is a scoring approach that uses the same training as the one-versus-one scoring method. In this case, each observation is scored only $k-1$ times, even though $k*(k-1)/2$ SVM models are trained. The training scheme for a four-class example is shown in Figure 11. In this illustration, a new observation starts at the top of the graph and is scored using the 1 vs. 4 SVM model. Then, depending on the outcome, the observation traverses the graph until it reaches one of the four class labels.

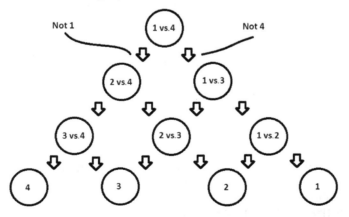

Figure 11. Directed Acyclic Graph Scoring Flow

The DAG method first runs the scoring from the one-versus-one SVM model that compared the first and last classes of the target (the order should be fixed, but the order does not matter). If the SVM model assigns the observation to the first class, then the last class can be ruled out. Thus the DAG method seeks to recursively exclude possible target class labels until only one label is left. That label becomes the class label for the new observation.

Each one-versus-one model is represented in the DAG. However, the number of times the observation is scored is only $k-1$, because as it is scored, it flows down the graph.

When you are using PROC HPSVM score code to run the DAG method, you need all the score code files from the one-versus-one training. To score recursively, you need to create two output data sets from each input set, in which you assign each observation to one of the two output data sets based on the predicted target class from the SVM model. SAS macro code to perform DAG scoring is presented in the SAS_SVM_DAG_SCORING macro in Appendix B.

EXPERIMENTS

This section presents a few brief examples that were run using the setup code in Appendix A and the macro code in Appendix B. All the runs of the HPSVM procedure use the procedure defaults, except that the kernel is chosen to be polynomial with degree 2 instead of linear, which is the default.

Table 1 lists the data sets that are used in the experiments. Many of these data sets are available in SAS Enterprise Miner. The **Wine** data set is from the UCI Machine Learning Repository (Lichman 2013).

Simulated data were created to run experiments with larger numbers of observations, input variables, and target classes. The target variable in the simulated data has approximately equal class sizes among the seven classes. In addition, only 9 of the 27 variables are correlated with the target levels, but these correlated variable also have large amounts of randomness.

The HPSVM procedure supports multithreading on a single machine as well as distributed computation. These experiments were run using a single desktop machine. Absolute times vary with hardware and setup, but the relative times provide important insight into how the different methods of multinomial classification compare with each other.

Data Set	Number of Observations	Number of Input Variables	Target Variable	Number of Target Classes	Location
Iris	150	4	Species	3	SASHELP.IRIS
Wine	178	13	Cultivar	3	UCI ML Repository
Cars	428	12	Type	6	SASHELP.CARS
German Credit	1000	20	employed	5	SAMPSIO.DMAGECR
Simulated 10K	10000	27	t	7	Simulated data

Table 1. Data Sets Used in the Experiments, along with Table Metadata

Table 2 shows the training and scoring times for each method on each data set. One-versus-one training is used for both one-versus-one scoring and DAG scoring. When the number of target classes is larger, such as in the **Cars** data set or the simulated data, the one-versus-one training requires more time to complete than the one-versus-all training. This is because there are $k*(k-1)/2$ models that require training for the one-versus-one method, compared to only k models for the one-versus-all method. The number of models that are trained is slightly offset by the fact that each of the models trained in the one-versus-one method uses fewer data than the models trained in the one-versus-all method, but as the number of target classes increases, the one-versus-one method takes more time.

Data Set	Training (sec)		Scoring (sec)		
	One-versus-All Method	One-versus-One Method	One-versus-All Method	One-versus-One Method	DAG Method
Iris	1	1	1	1	1
Wine	1	1	< 1	1	< 1
Cars	3	4	1	3	2
German Credit	11	7	1	3	2
Simulated 10K	67	76	2	7	5

Table 2. Timing for Running the Two Training and Three Scoring Methods on the Data Sets

Table 3 shows the misclassification rate for each data set and each scoring method. For each data set, the one-versus-one method has the best classification rate, followed very closely by the DAG method's classification rate. The one-versus-all method's classification rate is lower than that of the one-versus-one and DAG methods, especially on the larger data sets.

Data Set	One-versus-All Classification Rate (%)	One-versus-One Classification Rate (%)	DAG Classification Rate (%)
Iris	96.00	96.67	96.67
Wine	100	100	100
Cars	84.81	87.38	87.38
German Credit	72.5	76.6	76.3
Simulated 10K	70.07	78.06	78.04

Table 3. Classification Rate for Running the Three Different Scoring Methods on the Data Sets

CONCLUSION

This paper explains how to extend the HPSVM procedure for scoring multinomial targets. Two approaches to extending the SVM training are the one-versus-all and one-versus-one methods. When you are scoring the SVM model, you also have the option to use directed acyclic graphs (DAGs) to score the one-versus-one trained models.

The paper applies one-versus-all and one-versus-one training to several data sets to illustrate the strengths and weaknesses of the methods. The one-versus-one method does better at classifying observations than the one-versus-all method. This benefit is balanced by the fact that as the number of target classes increases, one-versus-one training takes longer than one-versus-all training. The scoring times are also longer for the one-versus-one and DAG methods than for the one-versus-all method. The DAG method runs faster than one-versus-one scoring, with only a marginal decrease in accuracy.

The paper also presents SAS macro code to perform the various multinomial classifications.

APPENDIX A

Before running the SAS macro code in Appendix B, you need to run the setup information. The following example does this for the **Iris** data set:

```
*** the training macros create several SAS data sets and some files;
*** to ensure that nothing is overwritten, create a new directory;
***     or point to an existing empty directory;
*** set the output directory below;
%let OutputDir = U:\SGF2017\; *change as needed;
x cd "&OutputDir";
libname l "&OutputDir";

*** set the target variable;
*** also set the input and score data sets;
*** you can change the score data every time you want to score new data;
%let Target    = Species; *case-sensitive;
%let InputData = sashelp.iris;
%let ScoreData = sashelp.iris;
proc contents data =&InputData out=names (keep = name type length);
run;
data names;
    set names;
    if name = "&Target" then do;
        call symput("TargetLength", length);
        delete;
    end;
run;
*** manually add names to interval or nominal type;
*** id variables are saved from the input data to the scored output data;
%let ID        = PetalLength PetalWidth SepalLength SepalWidth;
%let INPUT_NOM = ;
%let INPUT_INT = PetalLength PetalWidth SepalLength SepalWidth;
%let ID_NUM        = 4;
%let INPUT_NOM_NUM = 0;
%let INPUT_INT_NUM = 4;
*** PROC HPSVM options for the user (optional);
%let Maxiter   = 25;
%let Tolerance = 0.000001;
%let C         = 1;
```

APPENDIX B

The following macros include the one-versus-all training, one-versus-one training, one-versus-all scoring, one-versus-one scoring, and DAG scoring macros. The dummy variable creation is included in the one-versus-all and one-versus-one training macros and has been commented.

```
%macro SAS_SVM_ONE_VS_ALL_TRAIN();
*** separate the target for information-gathering purposes;
data l.TargetOnly;
    set &InputData;
    keep &Target;
    if MISSING(&Target) then delete;
run;
proc contents data = l.TargetOnly out=l.TType(keep = type);
run;
data _NULL_;
    set l.TType;
```

```
          call symput("TargetType", type);
run;
*** get the number of levels of the target;
proc freq data=l.TargetOnly nlevels;
    ods output nlevels=l.TargetNLevels OneWayFreqs=l.TargetLevels;
run;
*** create a variable, n, that is the number of levels of the target;
data _NULL_;
    set l.TargetNLevels;
    call symput("n", left(trim(nlevels)));
run;
*** create macro variables for each level of the target;
data _NULL_;
    set l.TargetLevels;
    i = _N_;
    call symput("level"||left(trim(i)), trim(left(right(&Target.))));
run;
*** create a column for each level of the target;
*** the value of the column is 1 if the target is that level, 0 otherwise;
data l.ModifiedInput;
    set &InputData;
    _MY_ID_ = _N_;
    %do i=1 %to &n;
        %if (&TargetType = 1) %then %do;
            if MISSING(&Target) then do;
                &Target.&&level&i = .;
              end;
            else if (&Target = &&level&i) then do;
                &Target.&&level&i = 1;
            end;
            else do;
                &Target.&&level&i = 0;
            end;
        %end;
        %else %if (&TargetType = 2) %then %do;
            if MISSING(&Target) then do;
                &Target.&&level&i = .;
              end;
            else if (&Target = "&&level&i") then do;
                &Target.&&level&i = 1;
            end;
            else do;
                &Target.&&level&i = 0;
            end;
        %end;
    %end;
run;
*** run an svm for each target. also save the scoring code for each svm;
%do i=1 %to &n;
    %let Target&i = &Target.&&level&i;

    data _NULL_;
        length svmcode $2000;
        svmcode  = "&OutputDir"!!"svmcode"!!"&i"!!".sas";
        call symput("svmcode"||left(trim(&i)), trim(svmcode));
    run;
```

```
        proc hpsvm data = l.ModifiedInput tolerance = &Tolerance c = &C
maxiter = &Maxiter nomiss;
        target &&Target&i;
        %if &INPUT_INT_NUM > 0 %then %do;
            input &INPUT_INT / level = interval;
        %end;
        %if &INPUT_NOM_NUM > 0 %then %do;
            input &INPUT_NOM / level = nominal;
        %end;
        *kernel linear;
        kernel polynomial / degree = 2;
        id _MY_ID_ &Target;
        code file = "&&svmcode&i";
    run;
%end;
*** this table lists all the svm scoring files;
data l.CodeInfoTable;
    length code $2000;
    %do i=1 %to &n;
        code = "&&svmcode&i";
        output;
    %end;
run;
%mend SAS_SVM_ONE_VS_ALL_TRAIN;


%macro SAS_SVM_ONE_VS_ONE_TRAIN();
*** separate the target for information-gathering purposes;
data l.TargetOnly;
    set &InputData;
    keep &Target;
    if MISSING(&Target) then delete;
run;
proc contents data = l.TargetOnly out=l.TType(keep = type);
run;
data _NULL_;
    set l.TType;
    call symput("TargetType", type);
run;
*** get the number of levels of the target;
proc freq data=l.TargetOnly nlevels;
    ods output nlevels=l.TargetNLevels OneWayFreqs=l.TargetLevels;
run;
*** create a variable, n, that is the number of levels of the target;
data _NULL_;
    set l.TargetNLevels;
    call symput("n", left(trim(nlevels)));
run;
*** create macro variables for each level of the target;
data _NULL_;
    set l.TargetLevels;
    i = _N_;
    call symput("level"||left(trim(i)), trim(left(right(&Target.))));
run;
*** create a column for each level of the target;
*** the value of the column is 1 if the target is that level, 0 otherwise;
data l.ModifiedInput;
```

```
        set &InputData;
        _MY_ID_ = _N_;
        %do i=1 %to &n;
            %if (&TargetType = 1) %then %do;
                if MISSING(&Target) then do;
                    &Target.&&level&i = .;
                end;
                else if (&Target = &&level&i) then do;
                    &Target.&&level&i = 1;
                end;
                else do;
                    &Target.&&level&i = 0;
                end;
            %end;
            %else %if (&TargetType = 2) %then %do;
                if MISSING(&Target) then do;
                    &Target.&&level&i = .;
                end;
                else if (&Target = "&&level&i") then do;
                    &Target.&&level&i = 1;
                end;
                else do;
                    &Target.&&level&i = 0;
                end;
            %end;
        %end;
run;
*** run an svm for each target. also save the scoring code for each svm;
%do i=1 %to &n;
    %do j=%eval(&i+1) %to &n;
        %let Target&i = &Target.&&level&i;
        %let Target&j = &Target.&&level&j;

        data _NULL_;
            length svmcode $2000;
            svmcode  = "&OutputDir"!!"svmcode"!!"&i"!!"_"!!"&j"!!".sas";
            call symput("svmcode&i._"||trim(left(&j)), trim(svmcode));
        run;

        proc hpsvm data = l.ModifiedInput(where=(&&Target&i=1 OR
&&Target&j=1)) tolerance = &Tolerance c = &C maxiter = &Maxiter nomiss;
            target &&Target&i;
            %if &INPUT_INT_NUM > 0 %then %do;
                input &INPUT_INT / level = interval;
            %end;
            %if &INPUT_NOM_NUM > 0 %then %do;
                input &INPUT_NOM / level = nominal;
            %end;
            *kernel linear;
            kernel polynomial / degree = 2;
            id _MY_ID_ &Target;
            code file = "&&svmcode&i._&j";
        run;
    %end;
%end;
*** this table lists all the svm scoring files;
data l.CodeInfoTable;
```

```
        length code $2000;
        %do i=1 %to &n;
            %do j=%eval(&i+1) %to &n;
                code = "&&svmcode&i._&j";
                output;
            %end;
        %end;
    run;
    %mend SAS_SVM_ONE_VS_ONE_TRAIN;


    %macro SAS_SVM_ONE_VS_ALL_SCORE();
    *** record the target type: 1 = numeric, 2 = character;
    data _NULL_;
        set l.TType;
        call symput("TargetType", type);
    run;
    *** create a variable, n, that is the number of levels of the target;
    data _NULL_;
        set l.TargetNLevels;
        call symput("n", left(trim(nlevels)));
    run;
    *** create macro variables for each level of the target;
    data _NULL_;
        set l.TargetLevels;
        i = _N_;
        call symput("level"||left(trim(i)), trim(left(right(&Target.))));
    run;
    *** read the code info table and create macro variables for each code
    file;
    data _NULL_;
        set l.CodeInfoTable;
        i = _N_;
        call symput("svmcode"||left(trim(i)), trim(left(right(code))));
    run;
    %do i=1 %to &n;
        %let Target&i = &Target.&&level&i;
    %end;
    *** score the data by using each score code;
    %MakeScoredOneVsAll();
    %mend SAS_SVM_ONE_VS_ALL_SCORE;

    %macro MakeScoredOneVsAll();
    data l.ScoredOutput;
        set &ScoreData;
        %if (&TargetType = 2) %then %do;
            length I_&Target $ &TargetLength;
        %end;
        %do i=1 %to &n;
            %inc "&&svmcode&i";
        %end;
        keep
        %do i=1 %to &n;
            P_&&Target&i..1
        %end;
        %if (&ID_NUM > 0) %then %do;
            &ID
```

```
        %end;
        I_&Target &Target;
        _P_ = 0;
        %do i=1 %to &n;
            %if (&TargetType = 1) %then %do;
                if (P_&&Target&i..1 > _P_) then do;
                    _P_ = P_&&Target&i..1;
                    I_&Target = &&level&i;
                end;
            %end;
            %else %if (&TargetType = 2) %then %do;
                if (P_&&Target&i..1 > _P_) then do;
                    _P_ = P_&&Target&i..1;
                    I_&Target = "&&level&i";
                end;
            %end;
        %end;
run;
%mend MakeScoredOneVsAll;


%macro SAS_SVM_ONE_VS_ONE_SCORE();
*** record the target type: 1 = numeric, 2 = character;
data _NULL_;
    set l.TType;
    call symput("TargetType", type);
run;
*** create a variable, n, that is the number of levels of the target;
data _NULL_;
    set l.TargetNLevels;
    call symput("n", left(trim(nlevels)));
run;
*** create macro variables for each level of the target;
data _NULL_;
    set l.TargetLevels;
    i = _N_;
    call symput("level"||left(trim(i)), trim(left(right(&Target.))));
run;
*** read the code info table and create macro variables for each code
file;
data _NULL_;
    set l.CodeInfoTable;
    i = _N_;
    call symput("svmcode"||left(trim(i)), trim(left(right(code))));
    call symput("numCode", i);
run;
%let k=1;
%do i=1 %to &n;
    %do j=%eval(&i+1) %to &n;
        %let svmcode&i._&j =&&svmcode&k;
        %let k =%eval(&k+1);
    %end;
%end;
%do i=1 %to &n;
    %let Target&i = &Target.&&level&i;
%end;
*** score the data by using each score code;
```

```sas
%MakeScoredOneVsOne();
%mend SAS_SVM_ONE_VS_ONE_SCORE;

%macro MakeScoredOneVsOne();
data l.ScoredOutput;
    set &ScoreData;
    %do k=1 %to &n;
        V_&&level&k = 0;
    %end;
    %if (&TargetType = 2) %then %do;
        length I_&Target $ &TargetLength;
    %end;
    %else %do;
        length I_&Target 8;
    %end;
run;
%do i=1 %to &n;
    %do j=%eval(&i+1) %to &n;
        data l.ScoredOutput;
            set l.ScoredOutput;
            %inc "&&svmcode&i._&j";
            if (P_&Target&&level&i..1 >= 0.5) then do;
                V_&&level&i = V_&&level&i+1;
            end;
            else do;
                V_&&level&j = V_&&level&j+1;
            end;
            _P_ = 0;
            %if (&TargetType = 1) %then %do;
                %do k=1 %to &n;
                    if (V_&&level&k > _P_) then do;
                        _P_ = V_&&level&k;
                        I_&Target = &&level&k;
                    end;
                %end;
            %end;
            %else %if (&TargetType = 2) %then %do;
                %do k=1 %to &n;
                    if (V_&&level&k > _P_) then do;
                        _P_ = V_&&level&k;
                        I_&Target = "&&level&k";
                    end;
                %end;
            %end;

            drop P_&Target&&level&i..1 P_&Target&&level&i..0
I_&Target&&level&i _P_;
        run;
    %end;
%end;
data l.ScoredOutput;
    set l.ScoredOutput;
    keep
    %do i=1 %to &n;
        V_&&level&i
    %end;
    %if (&ID_NUM > 0) %then %do;
```

```
            &ID
        %end;
        I_&Target &Target;
run;
%mend MakeScoredOneVsOne;


%macro SAS_SVM_DAG_SCORE();
*** record the target type: 1 = numeric, 2 = character;
data _NULL_;
    set l.TType;
    call symput("TargetType", type);
run;
*** create a variable, n, that is the number of levels of the target;
data _NULL_;
    set l.TargetNLevels;
    call symput("n", left(trim(nlevels)));
run;
*** create macro variables for each level of the target;
data _NULL_;
    set l.TargetLevels;
    i = _N_;
    call symput("level"||left(trim(i)), trim(left(right(&Target.))));
run;
*** read the code info table and create macro variables for each code
file;
data _NULL_;
    set l.CodeInfoTable;
    i = _N_;
    call symput("svmcode"||left(trim(i)), trim(left(right(code))));
    call symput("numCode", i);
run;
%let k=1;
%do i=1 %to &n;
    %do j=%eval(&i+1) %to &n;
        %let svmcode&i._&j =&&svmcode&k;
        %let k =%eval(&k+1);
    %end;
%end;
%do i=1 %to &n;
    %let Target&i = &Target.&&level&i;
%end;
*** score the data by using each score code;
%MakeScoredDAG();
%mend SAS_SVM_DAG_SCORE;

%macro MakeScoredDAG();
data ScoredOutput1_&n;
    set &ScoreData;
    _temp_IDvar_ensure_not_existing_ = _N_;
run;
%do k=1 %to %eval(&n-1);
    %let i=&k;
    %let j=&n;
    %do m=1 %to &k;
        %let left =%eval(&i+1);
        %let right=%eval(&j-1);
```

```
        data tempL tempR;
            set ScoredOutput&i._&j;
            %inc "&&svmcode&i._&j";
            if (I_&Target&&level&i = 1) then do;
                output tempR;
            end;
            else do;
                output tempL;
            end;
        run;
        %if &m=1 %then %do;
            data ScoredOutput&left._&j;
                set tempL;
            run;
        %end;
        %else %do;
            data ScoredOutput&left._&j;
                set ScoredOutput&left._&j tempL;
            run;
        %end;
        data ScoredOutput&i._&right;
            set tempR;
        run;
        %let i=%eval(&i-1);
        %let j=%eval(&j-1);
    %end;
%end;
data ScoredOutput;
    set
    %do i=1 %to &n;
        ScoredOutput&i._&i.(in = in&i.)
    %end;
    ;
    %if (&TargetType = 2) %then %do;
        length I_&Target $ &TargetLength;
    %end;
    %if (&TargetType = 1) %then %do;
        %do i=1 %to &n;
            if (in&i.) then do;
                I_&Target = &&level&i;
            end;
        %end;
    %end;
    %if (&TargetType = 2) %then %do;
        %do i=1 %to &n;
            if (in&i.) then do;
                I_&Target = "&&level&i";
            end;
        %end;
    %end;
    keep
    %if (&ID_NUM > 0) %then %do;
        &ID
    %end;
    I_&Target &Target _temp_IDvar_ensure_not_existing_;
run;
```

```
proc sort data=ScoredOutput
out=l.ScoredOutput(drop=_temp_IDvar_ensure_not_existing_);
    by _temp_IDvar_ensure_not_existing_;
run;
%do i=1 %to &n;
    %do j=&i %to &n;
        proc delete data=ScoredOutput&i._&j;
        run;
    %end;
%end;
%mend MakeScoredDAG;
```

REFERENCES

Cortes, C., and Vapnik, V. (1995). "Support-Vector Network." *Machine Learning* 20:273–297.

Hsu, C.-W., and Lin, C.-J. (2002). "A Comparison for Multiclass Support Vector Machines." *IEEE Transactions on Neural Networks* 13:415–425.

Lichman, M. (2013). "UCI Machine Learning Repository." School of Information and Computer Sciences, University of California, Irvine. http://archive.ics.uci.edu/ml.

Platt, J. C., Cristianini, N., and Shawe-Taylor, J. (2000). "Large Margin DAGs for Multiclass Classification." *Advances in Neural Information Processing Systems* 12:547–553.

CONTACT INFORMATION

Your comments and questions are valued and encouraged. Contact the authors:

Ralph Abbey
SAS Institute Inc.
Ralph.Abbey@sas.com

Taiping He
SAS Institute Inc.
Taiping.He@sas.com

Tao Wang
SAS Institute Inc.
T.Wang@sas.com

Factorization Machines: A New Tool for Sparse Data

Jorge Silva and Raymond E. Wright, SAS Institute Inc.

ABSTRACT

Factorization machines are a new type of model that is well suited to very high-cardinality, sparsely observed transactional data. This paper presents the new FACTMAC procedure, which implements factorization machines in SAS® Visual Data Mining and Machine Learning. This powerful and flexible model can be thought of as a low-rank approximation of a matrix or a tensor, and it can be efficiently estimated when most of the elements of that matrix or tensor are unknown. Thanks to a highly parallel stochastic gradient descent optimization solver, PROC FACTMAC can quickly handle data sets that contain tens of millions of rows. The paper includes examples that show you how to use PROC FACTMAC to recommend movies to users based on tens of millions of past ratings, predict whether fine food will be highly rated by connoisseurs, restore heavily damaged high-resolution images, and discover shot styles that best fit individual basketball players.

INTRODUCTION

Factorization models, which include factorization machines as a special case, are a broad class of models popular in statistics and machine learning. For example, principal component analysis is a well-known type of factorization model that has long been a staple of dimensionality reduction. For another example, matrix factorization has been widely used in text analysis and recommender systems. More recently, Rendle (2010, 2012) has proposed factorization machines for recommender systems and click-through rate prediction. Factorization machines are a powerful model that significantly extends matrix factorization.

Factorization machines are included in SAS Visual Data Mining and Machine Learning. The initial release supported matrix factorization with biases, and the latest implementation supports pairwise-interaction tensor factorization and nonnegative factorization. A macro is provided in the Appendix so that you can still perform pairwise-interaction tensor factorization even if you have PROC FACTMAC from the first release of SAS Visual Data Mining and Machine Learning.

This paper begins by briefly explaining the most relevant technical details of factorization machines for data scientists. Then it focuses on applications of factorization machines to solve real-world business problems. The application sections, which can be read by non-experts, include usage tips as well as code. The following application examples are presented:

- recommending movies to users based on tens of millions of past ratings
- predicting whether a fine food item will be highly rated by connoisseurs
- restoring heavily damaged high-resolution images
- discovering shot styles that best fit individual basketball players

From these examples, you will learn how to spot which types of problems are good candidates for factorization machines, how to prepare data for PROC FACTMAC, how to score new data by using score code or PROC ASTORE, and what strategies to use for choosing parameters and training the best factorization machine models.

THE FACTORIZATION MACHINE MODEL

This section begins with a brief mathematical description of factorization machines. Assuming a training set $D = \{(x_i, y_i)\}$, with $i = 1, \ldots, n$, where x_i refers to the ith observation and y_i refers to the ith target value, the factorization machine model of order 2 is written as

$$\hat{y}(x) = w_0 + \sum_{j=1}^{p} w_j x_j + \sum_{j=1}^{p} \sum_{j'=1}^{p} x_j x_{j'} \sum_{f=1}^{k} v_{jf} v_{j'f}$$

where $x = (x_1, \dots, x_p)$ is an observed p-dimensional input feature vector, $\hat{y}$ is the predicted target,

w_0 is a global bias, w_j are per-feature biases, and v_{jf} denotes coordinate f of the k-dimensional factor vector v_j.

The overall factor matrix V of size $p \times k$ is the concatenation of the row vectors v_j for $j = 1, \dots, p$.

The number of factors is k. The model parameters to be estimated are $w_0, w_1, \dots, w_p$ and V.

The estimation is done by minimizing the root mean square error (RMSE), which is defined as

$$\text{RMSE} = \sqrt{\frac{1}{n} \sum_{i=1}^{n} (\hat{y}(x_i) - y_i)^2}$$

over the training set D.

Interestingly, it is known that factorization machines approximate polynomial-kernel support vector machines and are more resistant to overfitting when the design matrix is sparse (Rendle 2010).

FACTORIZATION MACHINES FOR RECOMMENDATIONS

Recommender systems are a diverse class of algorithms that aim to learn user preferences in order to recommend items such as movies, books, or songs. The purpose is to predict which ratings a user would hypothetically give to a set of items and then to recommend items that the user is likely to prefer the most. As illustrated in Figure 1, users and items form a matrix. This matrix is potentially very large, because there can be millions of users and items. Moreover, it is very sparsely observed, because usually only a very small fraction of historical ratings are available.

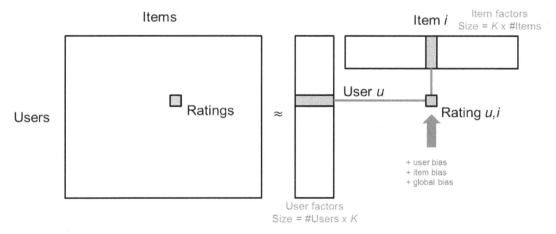

Figure 1. Matrix factorization for a recommender system. Users and items are characterized by their respective *k*-dimensional factor vectors.

You can overcome these challenges by factorizing the matrix into lower-dimensional user and item factors, which can be used to predict new ratings. For recommender systems, the input vector is typically constructed using binary indicator variables for user u and item i, as illustrated in Figure 2.

$$x = (\underbrace{0, ..., 0, 1, 0, ..., 0}_{|U|}, \underbrace{0, ..., 0, 1, 0, ..., 0}_{|I|})$$

Figure 2. Input vector for recommender systems.

The factorization machine model is then equivalent to the following equation for predicting new ratings:

$$\hat{y}(x) = \hat{y}(u, i) = w_0 + w_u + w_i + \sum_{f=1}^{k} v_{uf} v_{if}$$

EXAMPLE: RECOMMENDING MOVIES

This example draws on data that are derived from companies that provide movies for online viewing. A company wants to offer its customers recommendations of movies that they might like. These recommendations are based on ratings that users provide.The `MovieLens` data set, which contains movie ratings, was developed by the GroupLens project at the University of Minnesota and is available at http://grouplens.org/datasets/movielens (Harper and Konstan 2015). This example uses the `MovieLens` 100K version.

The `MovieLens` 100K data set has four columns: user ID, item ID (each item is a movie), timestamp, and rating. This example predicts the rating for a specified user ID and an item ID. The data set is very sparse because most combinations of users and movies are not rated.

You can download the compressed archive file from the URL http://files.grouplens.org/datasets/movielens/ml-100k.zip and use any third-party unzip tool to extract all the files from the archive and store them in the destination directory of your choice. The file that contains the ratings is named `u.data`. Assuming that your destination directory is `~/data`, the following DATA step loads the data table from the directory into your CAS session:

```
proc casutil;
    load file="~/data/u.data"     /*or other user-defined location*/
    casout="movlens"
    importoptions=(filetype="CSV" delimiter="TAB" getnames="FALSE"
                vars=("userid" "itemid" "rating" "timestamp"));
run;
```

The following statements show how to use PROC FACTMAC to predict movie ratings:

```
proc factmac data=mycas.movlens nfactors=10 learnstep=0.15
                                maxiter=20  outmodel=factors;

    input userid itemid /level=nominal;
    target rating /level=interval;
    output out=mycas.out1 copyvars=(userid itemid rating);
run;
```

The NFACTORS parameter corresponds to k in the model equations. The LEARNSTEP parameter is an optimization parameter that controls how fast the stochastic gradient descent solver learns. Smaller values increase accuracy but might require a larger number of iterations to reach a good solution.

The following statements print the first 10 observations in the `Factors` data table, which is specified in the OUTMODEL= option in the PROC FACTMAC statement. The output is shown in Figure 3.

```
proc print data=factors(obs=10);
run;
```

Obs	Variable	Level	Bias	Factor1	Factor2	Factor3	Factor4	Factor5	Factor6	Factor7	Factor8	Factor9	Factor10
1	_GLOBAL_		3.52986	0.00000	0.00000	0.00000	0.00000	0.00000	0.00000	0.00000	0.00000	0.00000	0.00000
2	userid	1	0.08043	0.26696	-0.01986	0.08144	-0.41570	-0.52615	0.28814	-0.11806	-0.00410	-0.17100	-0.05212
3	userid	2	0.17982	0.07208	0.22698	0.29656	0.00968	0.31132	0.20286	-0.04221	-0.29003	-0.40891	0.08394
4	userid	3	-0.73356	0.02376	0.77677	-0.35886	0.72389	0.11038	-0.00465	-1.01402	-0.01799	-0.19742	-0.59410
5	userid	4	0.80347	0.14017	0.20294	-1.15726	-0.34206	0.56472	-0.31749	0.05059	-0.35566	0.53735	-0.39922
6	userid	5	-0.65557	0.26512	0.59145	1.11076	0.21193	-0.86156	0.40307	-0.12330	0.08508	0.09446	-0.15703
7	userid	6	0.10521	0.28837	-0.34583	0.25138	0.03088	0.63992	-0.36136	-0.84011	-0.05914	-0.09977	0.37007
8	userid	7	0.43540	-0.48234	0.38773	0.38406	-0.03201	0.37931	0.48041	-0.16691	0.13510	0.24185	-0.09080
9	userid	8	0.26675	0.07745	0.66465	-0.21473	-0.34774	0.14239	0.58124	-0.66962	0.40012	-0.37498	-0.64648
10	userid	9	0.74287	0.64185	0.26543	-0.56766	-0.35184	-0.43720	0.73286	0.23230	0.30744	0.43841	0.72421

Figure 3. Factors data table for the MovieLens data set.

When the model is saved in the `mycaslib.astore` data table, you can predict new ratings by using the ASTORE procedure, as in the following statements:

```
proc astore;
   score data = mycaslib.valid
   out=mycaslib.ScoreValid copyvar = rating
   rstore = mycaslib.astore;
run;
```

The first 20 predicted ratings are shown in Figure 4.

Obs	userid	itemid	rating	P_rating
1	196	242	3	4.77726
2	186	302	3	3.20633
3	22	377	1	1.31919
4	244	51	2	3.13430
5	166	346	1	1.94193
6	298	474	4	4.72592
7	115	265	2	3.15252
8	253	465	5	3.93033
9	305	451	3	2.99026
10	6	86	3	3.83011
11	62	257	2	3.70526
12	286	1014	5	3.42622
13	200	222	5	4.19948
14	210	40	3	3.58510
15	224	29	3	2.72739
16	303	785	3	2.58885
17	122	387	5	4.31811
18	194	274	2	2.55058
19	291	1042	4	3.34704
20	234	1184	2	2.76020

Figure 4. Predicted movie ratings. The predictions are in the P_rating column.

EXAMPLE: RECOMMENDING FINE FOODS

In this example, you can use PROC FACTMAC to analyze fine food reviews. The Amazon Fine Foods data set, available at https://snap.stanford.edu/data/web-FineFoods.html, consists of ratings and text reviews of gourmet foods sold by Amazon (Leskovec and Krevl 2014). The data span a period of more than 10 years, including all ~500,000 reviews up to October 2012. The data include product and user information, ratings, and a plaintext review.

The input variables are product/productId, review/userId, review/profileName, review/helpfulness, review/score, review/time, review/summary and review/text. Here is an example of content in the review/text field:

I have bought several of the Vitality canned dog food products and have found them all to be of good quality. The product looks more like a stew than a processed meat and it smells better. My Labrador is finicky and she appreciates this product better than most.

Unlike the data set in the movie recommendation example, this data set include more than two nominal input variables. In this situation, the factorization machine model is equivalent to the following pairwise-interaction tensor factorization equation:

$$\hat{y}(\boldsymbol{x}) = \hat{y}(user, product, time, helpfulness)$$
$$= w_0 + w_{user} + w_{product} + w_{time} + w_{helpfulness}$$
$$+\langle \boldsymbol{v}_{user}, \boldsymbol{v}_{product}\rangle + \langle \boldsymbol{v}_{user}, \boldsymbol{v}_{time}\rangle + \cdots + \langle \boldsymbol{v}_{user}, \boldsymbol{v}_{helpfulness}\rangle$$

This model considers every interaction between pairs of input variables. Although you might find this equation cumbersome, the corresponding PROC FACTMAC syntax is actually quite simple to specify. After importing the data into SAS, you can train the model by using the following code:

```
proc factmac data=mycas.amazon_foods
   nFactors=20 learnStep=0.01 maxIter=50 outModel=mycas.factors;
   input userId productId time helpfulness /level=nominal;
   target reviewScore /level=interval;
   output out=mycas.out1 copyvars=(userId productId time helpfulness);
run;
```

If you have PROC FACTMAC from the initial release of SAS Visual Data Mining and Machine Learning, you can alternatively use the following code:

```
%pairwiseFactMac(inputVarList=userId productId time helpfulness,

              target=reviewScore,

              dataset=amazon_foods,

              maxIter=50,

              nFactors=20,

              learnStep=0.01,

              configFile=);
```

The pairwiseFactMac macro is provided in the Appendix at the end of this paper.

The model achieves an RMSE of 0.91, which is competitive with other methods. You can visit https://github.com/sassoftware/enlighten-apply for additional code snippets and tips for incorporating the text of the reviews into the analysis. Interestingly, the Amazon Fine Food reviews are overwhelmingly positive, and coffee is by far the most popular product, well ahead of chocolate.

FACTORIZATION MACHINES FOR IMAGE RECONSTRUCTION

In image processing, it is sometimes necessary to perform reconstruction based on damaged copies of an image. You can use PROC FACTMAC for this purpose, by using the following code example:

```
proc factmac data=mycaslib.sparsePixels

   outmodel=factors

   maxiter=500

   nfactors=100

   learnstep=0.01

   seed=12345;

   input x y  /level=nominal;

   target pixelValue /level=interval;

   output out=mycaslib.FactMacScore copyvar = (x y pixelValue);

run;
```

The `sparsePixels` data table consists of three columns: x, y, and pixelValue. Each row corresponds to a nonmissing pixel. The results are shown in Figure 5. In this example, the corrupted image has 50% missing pixels.

Note that factorization machines are suitable for imputing many other types of data besides images.

Figure 5. Image reconstruction. Left: Original image. Center: 50% missing pixels. Right: Image reconstructed using PROC FACTMAC.

FACTORIZATION MACHINES FOR PREDICTIVE MODELING IN BASKETBALL

The data for this example consist of basketball shots recorded during the 2015–2016 NBA season, from October 2015 through March 2016. The data set was downloaded using the API available from Sportradar.com. Every shot taken by every player is recorded, excluding free throws. Figure 6 shows how shot success varies by where on the court the shot was taken and whether the player is a center, forward, or guard.

The input variables that are used for the analysis are player_name, action_type, shot_zone_area, and shot_zone_range. The target variable is constructed by computing the log-odds of shot success per player.

In this example, as in the food reviews example, there are more than two nominal variables. Hence, you can perform pairwise-interaction tensor factorization.

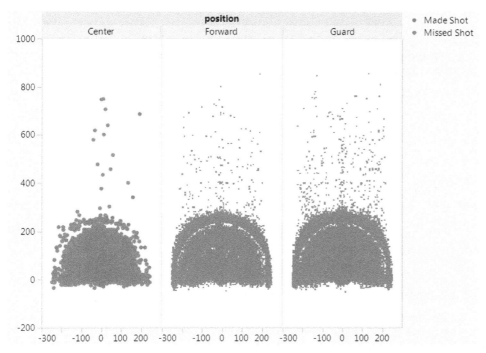

Figure 6. Shot success by court location and player position. Data from Sportradar.com.

The following code performs pairwise-interaction tensor factorization for this data set:

```
proc factmac data=mycaslib.nbaShooting_summarized
    outmodel=factors
    maxiter=50
    nfactors=10
    learnstep=0.03
    input player_name action_type shot_zone_area shot_zone_range
            /level=nominal;
    target logit /level=interval;
    output out=mycaslib.ScoreTrain copyvar=logit;
    savestate rstore=mycaslib.astore;
run;
```

You can score a held-out data set by using the following statements:

```
proc astore;
    score data = mycaslib.valid
    out=mycaslib.ScoreValid&i copyvar = (&target.)
    rstore = mycaslib.astore&i.;
run;
```

Alternatively, if PROC FACTMAC in your release of SAS Visual Data Mining and Machine Learning does not support tensor factorization, you can use the following code to perform pairwise-interaction tensor factorization and score a held-out validation data set:

```
%pairwiseFactMac(inputVarList=player_name action_type shot_zone_area
                 shot_zone_range,
          target=logit,
          dataset=ray.nbaShooting_Summarized,
          maxIter=50,
          nFactors=10,
          learnStep=0.03,
          configFile=);
```

The pairwiseFactMac macro is provided in the Appendix at the end of this paper.

In addition to achieving an RMSE value of 0.93, which favorably compares to 1.39 for a support vector machine used with the same data, the factorization machine analysis reveals multiple insights. The following action types are most associated with shot success (they have the highest estimated bias values):

- running dunk shot
- running layup
- driving layup
- alley-oop dunk shot
- dunk shot
- cutting dunk shot
- putback layup
- driving dunk shot
- tip dunk shot
- driving dunk shot

As you can see, a large proportion of these action types are dunk shots. In contrast, the following action types are most associated with shot failure:

- turnaround hook shot
- turnaround jump shot
- fadeaway jump shot
- driving floating layup
- turnaround fadeaway shot
- running jump shot
- hook shot

- step-back jump shot

- pull-up jump shot

- jump shot

These action types are known to represent difficult, acrobatic shots. In addition, Figure 7 shows a visualization of the player and action factor vectors on the same plot. Because these are high-dimensional vectors, a 2D visualization is created using the t-distributed stochastic neighbor embedding (t-SNE) method (Van der Maaten and Hinton 2008). Blue points are actions, and red points are players. Similar shots appear close together, as do players who have similar shot profiles (such as Kobe Bryant and Russell Westbrook). Also, it appears from the figure that Manu Ginobili is proficient at driving floating layups, because his latent factor vector is embedded very near that of the corresponding action.

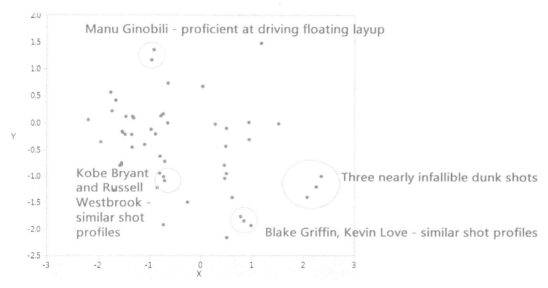

Figure 7. Visualization of player (red) and action (blue) factors. Data from Sportradar.com.

CONCLUSION

The FACTMAC procedure implements factorization machines in SAS Visual Data Mining and Machine Learning. This new model enables you to solve a variety of tasks, from recommendation to predictive modeling and image processing, all of which involve sparse data. Thanks to a highly parallel optimization solver, PROC FACTMAC can handle very large data sets. This powerful and flexible method provides not only predictions but also meaningful factor representations that can give you insights into many types of business problems.

REFERENCES

Harper, F. M., and Konstan, J. A. (2015). "The MovieLens Datasets: History and Context." *ACM Transactions on Interactive Intelligent Systems (TiiS)* 5:19 pages. http://dx.doi.org/10.1145/2827872.

Leskovec, J., and Krevl, A. (2014). SNAP Datasets: Stanford Large Network Dataset Collection. https://snap.stanford.edu/data.

Rendle, S. (2010). "Factorization Machines." *In Proceedings of the 10th IEEE International Conference on Data Mining (ICDM).* Piscataway, NJ: Institute of Electrical And Electronics Engineers.

Rendle, S. (2012). "Factorization Machines with libFM." *ACM Transactions on Intelligent Systems and Technology* 3:1–22.

Sportradar AG. (2017). Sportradar.com. St. Gallen, Switzerland.

Van der Maaten, L. J. P., and Hinton, G. E. (2008). "Visualizing Data Using t-SNE." *Journal of Machine Learning Research* 9:2579–2605.

APPENDIX

The following macro implements pairwise-interaction tensor factorization by combining multiple pairwise factorization machine models.

```
%macro pairwisefactMac(
    inputVarList=,
    target=,
    dataset=,
    partitionFraction=.7,
    maxIter=100,
    nFactors=25,
    learnStep=0.10,
    configFile=
);


%let nInputs = %sysfunc(countw(&inputVarList.));
%put nInputs = &nInputs.;
%let k = 2; /*k=2 requests pairs*/


%let nCombo = %sysfunc(comb(&nInputs.,&k.));
%put nCombo = &nCombo.;


%let listQuoted = ;

*identify each pair inputs;
data pairs (keep=pairs);
    length pairs $65.;
    array V{&nInputs.} $32 (

        /*quote each input*/
        %do i = 1 %to &nInputs.;
            %let currentVar = %scan(&inputVarList.,&i.);
```

```
                                        "&currentVar."
                        %end;
            );


                do j=1 to &nCombo.;
                    call allcomb(j,&k.,of V[*]);
                    do i = 1 to &k.;
                        if i=1 then
                        do;
                                        pairs="";
                            counter=0;
                        end;
                        counter=counter+1;
                        pairs=cat(compress(pairs),' ',compress(V[i]));
                        if counter=&k. then output;
                    end;
                end;
    run;


*save pairs as macro variables;
data _null_;
        set pairs end = eof;
    call symput ('pair'||strip(_n_),pairs);
    run;


*call proc factmac, looping over the pairs;
libname mycaslib sasioca ;


data mycaslib.train mycaslib.valid;
        set &dataset.;
        if ranuni(0) le &partitionFraction. then output mycaslib.train;
            else output mycaslib.valid;
    run;


%do i = 1 %to &nCombo.;
        proc factmac data=mycaslib.train
                maxiter=&maxIter.
```

12

```
                nfactors=&nFactors.
                learnstep=&learnStep.;
                input &&pair&i. /level=nominal;
                target &target. /level=interval;
                output out=mycaslib.ScoreTrain&i. copyvar = (&target.);
                savestate rstore=mycaslib.astore&i.;
        run;

        proc astore;
        score data = mycaslib.valid
        out=mycaslib.ScoreValid&i copyvar = (&target.)
                rstore = mycaslib.astore&i.;
        run;
    %end;


    data mycaslib.ScoreTrain;
        merge
        %do i = 1 %to &nCombo.;
                mycaslib.ScoreTrain&i. (rename=(p_&target. =
p_&target._&i.))
            %end;
        ;
        _partInd_ = 1;
    run;


    data mycaslib.ScoreValid;
        merge
        %do i = 1 %to &nCombo.;
                mycaslib.ScoreValid&i. (rename=(p_&target. =
p_&target._&i.))
            %end;
        ;


        _partInd_ = 0;
    run;


    data mycaslib.ScoreCombined;
        set mycaslib.ScoreTrain
```

```
                    mycaslib.ScoreValid
        ;
    run;


    *build a regression model to predict target using predicted values for all
pairs;
    proc regselect  data = mycaslib.scoreCombined;
        model &target.=
          %do i=1 %to &nCombo.;
                    p_&target._&i.
            %end;
        ;
        partition rolevar=_partInd_ (TRAIN="1" VALIDATE="0");
    run;
    quit;
%mend pairwiseFactMac;
```

CONTACT INFORMATION

Your comments and questions are valued and encouraged. Contact the author at:

Jorge Silva
jorge.silva@sas.com

Building Bayesian Network Classifiers Using the HPBNET Procedure Ye Liu, Weihua Shi, and Wendy Czika, SAS Institute Inc.

ABSTRACT

A Bayesian network is a directed acyclic graphical model that represents probability relationships and conditional independence structure between random variables. SAS® Enterprise Miner™ implements a Bayesian network primarily as a classification tool; it supports naïve Bayes, tree-augmented naïve Bayes, Bayesian-network-augmented naïve Bayes, parent-child Bayesian network, and Markov blanket Bayesian network classifiers. The HPBNET procedure uses a score-based approach and a constraint-based approach to model network structures. This paper compares the performance of Bayesian network classifiers to other popular classification methods such as classification tree, neural network, logistic regression, and support vector machines. The paper also shows some real-world applications of the implemented Bayesian network classifiers and a useful visualization of the results.

INTRODUCTION

Bayesian network (BN) classifiers are one of the newest supervised learning algorithms available in SAS Enterprise Miner. The HP BN Classifier node is a high-performance data mining node that you can select from the HPDM toolbar; it uses the HPBNET procedure in SAS® High-Performance Data Mining to learn a BN structure from a training data set. This paper show how the various BN structures that are available in PROC HPBNET can be used as a predictive model for classifying a binary or nominal target.

Because of the practical importance of classification, many other classifiers besides BN classifiers are commonly applied. These classifiers include logistic regression, decision tree, support vector machines, and neural network classifiers. Recent research in supervised learning has shown that the prediction performance of the BN classifiers is competitive when compared to these other classifiers. However, BN classifiers can surpass these competitors in terms of interpretability. A BN can explicitly represent distributional dependency relationships among all available random variables; thus it enables you to discover and interpret the dependency and causality relationships among variables in addition to the target's conditional distribution. In contrast, support vector machines and neural network classifiers are black boxes and logistic regression and decision tree classifiers only estimate the conditional distribution of the target. Therefore, BN classifiers have great potential in real-world classification applications, especially in fields where interpretability is a concern.

SAS Enterprise Miner implements PROC HPBNET to build BN classifiers that can take advantage of modern multithreaded distributed-computing platforms. The HPBNET procedure can build five types of BN classifiers: naïve BN, tree-augmented naïve BN, BN-augmented naïve BN, parent-child BN, and Markov blanket BN. This paper introduces the basic structure of these five types of BN classifiers, explains the key programming techniques and outputs of the HPBNET procedure, and demonstrates useful visualization methods for displaying the structures of the output BN classifiers. This paper also compares the prediction performance of BN classifiers to that of the previously mentioned competitor classifiers by using 25 data sets in the UCI Machine Learning Repository (Lichman 2013).

A Bayesian network is a graphical model that consists of two parts, <**G, P**>:

- **G** is a directed acyclic graph (DAG) in which nodes represent random variables and arcs between nodes represent conditional dependency of the random variables.

- **P** is a set of conditional probability distributions, one for each node conditional on its parents.

The following example explains these terms in greater detail.

EXAMPLE OF A SIMPLE BAYESIAN NETWORK

Figure 1 shows a Bayesian network for a house alarm from Russell and Norvig (2010). It describes the following scenario: Your house has an alarm system against burglary. You live in a seismically active area, and the alarm system can be set off occasionally by an earthquake. You have two neighbors, Mary and John, who do not know each other. If they hear the alarm, they might or might not call you.

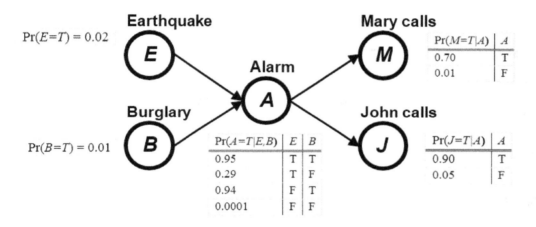

Figure 1. House Alarm Bayesian Network

In the house alarm Bayesian network, E, B, A, M, and J are called nodes, and the links between those five nodes are called edges or arcs. Node A is the parent of nodes J and M because the links point from A to J and M; nodes J and M are called the children of node A. Similarly, nodes E and B are the parents of node A; node A is the child of nodes E and B. Those nodes and edges constitute the graph (**G**) part of the Bayesian network model. The conditional probability tables (CPTs) that are associated with the nodes are the probability distribution (**P**) part of the Bayesian network model.

PROPERTIES OF BAYESIAN NETWORK

Two important properties of a Bayesian network are the following:

- Edges (arcs between nodes) represent "causation," so no directed cycles are allowed.

- Each node is conditionally independent of its ancestors given its parents. This is called Markov property.

According to the Markov property, the joint probability distribution of all nodes in the network can be factored to the product of the conditional probability distributions of each node given its parents. That is,

$$Pr(G) = Pr(X_1, X_2, ..., X_p) = \prod_{i=1}^{p} Pr(X_i | \pi(X_i))$$

where $\pi(X_i)$ are the parents of node X_i.

In the simplest case, where all the X_i are discrete variables as in the following example, conditional distribution is represented as CPTs, each of which lists the probability that the child node takes on each of its different values for each combination of values of its parents.

In the house alarm example, observe that whether Mary or John calls is conditionally dependent only on the state of the alarm (that is, their parent node). Based on the graph, the joint probability distribution of the events (E, B, A, M, and J) is

$$Pr(E, B, A, M, J) = Pr(J|A) \cdot Pr(M|A) \cdot Pr(A|E, B) \cdot Pr(B) \cdot Pr(E)$$

The network structure together with the conditional probability distributions completely determine the Bayesian network model.

SUPERVISED LEARNING USING A BAYESIAN NETWORK MODEL

Now consider this question:

> Suppose you are at work, the house is burglarized (B = True), there is no earthquake (E = False), your neighbor Mary calls to say your alarm is ringing (M = True), but neighbor John doesn't call (J = False). What is the probability that the alarm went off (A = True)?

In other words, what is the value of

$$Pr(A = T | B = T, E = F, M = T, J = F)$$

To simplify the appearance of these equations, T and F are used to represent True and False, respectively.

From the definition of conditional probability,

$$Pr(A = T | B = T, E = F, M = T, J = F) = \frac{Pr(A = T, B = T, E = F, M = T, J = F)}{Pr(B = T, E = F, M = T, J = F)}$$

According to the equation for $Pr(E, B, A, M, J)$ from the preceding section and using the values from the conditional probability tables that are shown in Figure 1,

$Pr(A = T, B = T, E = F, M = T, J = F)$
$= Pr(J = F|A = T) \, Pr(M = T|A = T) Pr(A = T|E = F, B = T) Pr(B = T) Pr(E = F)$
$= 0.1 * 0.01 * 0.7 * 0.94 * (1 - 0.02) = 0.00064484$

$Pr(B = T, E = F, M = T, J = F) = Pr(A = T, B = T, E = F, M = T, J = F) + Pr(A = F, B = T, E = F, M = T, J = F)$
$= 0.00064484 + Pr(A = F, B = T, E = F, M = T, J = F)$
$= 0.00064484$
$+ Pr(J = F|A = F) \, Pr(B = T) \, Pr(M = T|A = F) \, Pr(A = F|E = F, B = T) \, Pr(E = F)$
$= 0.00064484 + (1 - 0.05) * 0.01 * 0.01 * (1 - 0.94) * (1 - 0.02) = 0.000650426$

$Pr(A = T|B = T, E = F, M = T, J = F) = \dfrac{0.00064484}{0.000650426} \approx 0.99$

Thus, the conditional probability of the alarm having gone off in this situation is about 0.99. This value can be used to classify (predict) whether the alarm went off.

In general, based on a Bayesian network model, a new observation $X = (x_1, x_2, ..., x_p)$ is classified by determining the classification of the target Y that has the largest conditional probability,

$$\arg \max_k \Pr(Y = k | x_1, x_2, ..., x_p)$$

where

$$\Pr(Y = k | x_1, x_2, ..., x_p) \propto \Pr(Y = k, x_1, x_2, ..., x_p) = \prod_i \Pr(x_i | \pi(X_i)) Pr(Y = k | \pi(Y))$$

Because the target is binary (True or False) in this example, when the value of the preceding equation is greater than 0.5, the prediction is that the alarm went off (A = True).

HPBNET PROCEDURE

The HPBNET procedure is a high-performance procedure that can learn different types of Bayesian networks—naïve, tree-augmented naïve (TAN), Bayesian network-augmented naïve (BAN), parent-child Bayesian network (PC), or Markov blanket (MB)—from an input data set. PROC HPBNET runs in either single-machine mode or distributed-computing mode. In this era of big data, where computation performance is crucial for many real-world applications, the HPBNET procedure's distributed-computing mode is very efficient in processing large data sets.

The HPBNET procedure supports two types of variable selection: one by independence tests between each input variable and the target (when PRESCREENING=1), and the other by conditional independence tests between each input variable and the target given any subset of other input variables (when VARSELECT=1, 2, or 3). PROC HPBNET uses specialized data structures to efficiently compute the contingency tables for any variable combination, and it uses dynamic candidate generation to reduce the number of false candidates for variable combinations. If you have many input variables, structure learning can be time-consuming because the number of variable combinations is exponential. Therefore, variable selection is strongly recommended.

To learn a TAN structure, the HPBNET procedure constructs a maximum spanning tree in which the weight for an edge is the mutual information between the two nodes. A maximum spanning tree is a spanning tree of a weighted graph that has maximum weight. If there are K variables in a system, then the corresponding tree structure will have K nodes, and K−1 edges should be added to create a tree structure that connects all the nodes in the graph. Also, the sum of the weights of all the edges needs to be the maximum weight among all such tree structures.

To learn the other BN types, PROC HPBNET uses both of the following approaches:

- The score-based approach uses the BIC (Bayesian information criterion) score to measure how well a structure fits the training data and then tries to find the structure that has the best score. The BIC is defined as

$$\text{BIC}(G, D) = N \sum_{i=1}^{n} \sum_{j=1}^{q_i} \sum_{k=1}^{r_i} p(\pi_{ij}) p(X_i = v_{ik} | \pi_{ij}) \ln p(X_i = v_{ik} | \pi_{ij}) - \frac{M}{2} \ln N$$

    where G is a network, D is the training data set, N is the number of observations in D, n is the number of variables, X_i is a random variable, r_i is the number of levels for X_i, v_{ik} is the kth value of X_i, q_i is the number of value combinations of X_i's parents, π_{ij} is the jth value combination of X_i's parents, and $M = \sum_{i=1}^{n}(r_i - 1) \times q_i$ is the number of parameters for the probability distributions.

- The constraint-based approach uses independence tests (such as a chi-square test or mutual information test) to determine the edges and directions among the nodes as follows: Assume that you have three variables, X, Y and Z, and that it has been determined (using independence tests) that there are edges between X and Z and Y and Z, but no edge between X and Y. If X is conditionally independent of Y given any subset of variables $S = \{Z\} \cup S'$, $S' \subseteq \{X, Y, Z\}$, then the directions between X and Z and between Y and Z are $X \rightarrow Z$ and $Y \rightarrow Z$, respectively. Notice that using only independence tests might not be able to orient all edges because some structures are equivalent with respect to conditional independence tests. For example, $X \leftarrow Y \leftarrow Z$, $X \rightarrow Y \rightarrow Z$, and $X \leftarrow Y \rightarrow Z$ belong to the same equivalence class. In these cases, PROC HPBNET uses the BIC score to determine the directions of the edges.

For the PC and MB structures, PROC HPBNET learns the parents of the target first. Then it learns the parents of the input variable that has the highest BIC score with the target. It continues learning the parents of the input variable that has the next highest BIC score, and so on. When learning the parents of a node, it first determines the edges by using independence tests. Then it orients the edges by using both independence tests and the BIC score. PROC HPBNET uses the BIC score not only for orienting the edges but also for controlling the network complexity, because a complex network that has more parents is penalized in the BIC score. Both the BESTONE and BESTSET values of the PARENTING= option try to find the local optimum structure for each node. BESTONE adds the best candidate variable to the parents at each iteration, whereas BESTSET tries to choose the best set of variables among the candidate sets.

TYPES OF BAYESIAN NETWORK CLASSIFIERS SUPPORTED BY THE HPBNET PROCEDURE

The HPBNET procedure supports the following types of Bayesian network classifiers:

- **Naïve Bayesian network classifier:** As shown in Figure 2, the target node (Y) has a direct edge to each input variable, the target node is the only parent for all other nodes, and there are no other edges. This structure assumes that all input variables are conditionally independent of each other given the target.

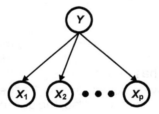

Figure 2. Naïve Bayesian Network Classifier

- **Tree-augmented naïve Bayesian network classifier:** As shown in Figure 3, in addition to the edges from the target node Y to each input node, the edges among the input nodes form a tree. This structure is less restrictive than the naïve Bayes structure.

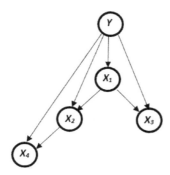

Figure 3. Tree-Augmented Naïve Bayesian Network Classifier

- **Bayesian network-augmented naïve Bayesian network classifier:** As shown in Figure 4, the target node Y has a direct edge to each input node, and the edges among the input nodes form a Bayesian network.

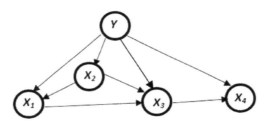

Figure 4. Bayesian Network-Augmented Naïve Bayesian Network Classifier

- **Parent-child Bayesian network classifier:** As shown in Figure 5, input variables can be the parents of the target variable Y. In addition, edges from the parents of the target to the children of the target and among the children of the target are also possible.

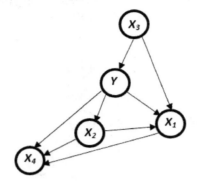

Figure 5. Parent-Child Bayesian Network Classifier

- **Markov blanket Bayesian network classifier:** As shown in Figure 6, the Markov blanket includes the target's parents, children, and spouses (the other parents of the target's children).

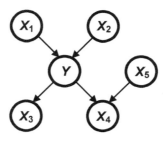

Figure 6. Markov Blanket Bayesian Network Classifier

One advantage of PROC HPBNET is that you can specify all the structures that you want to consider for training and request (by specifying the BESTMODEL option) that the procedure automatically choose the best structure based on each model's performance on validation data.

EXAMPLE OF USING PROC HPBNET TO ANALYZE DATA

This example uses PROC HPBNET to diagnose whether a patient has breast cancer, based on the Breast Cancer Wisconsin data set from the UCI Machine Learning Repository (Lichman 2013).

Table 1 lists the details of the attributes found in this data set.

Variables	Attribute	Domain	Description of Benign Cells	Description of Cancerous Cells
1	Sample code number	ID number	N/A	N/A
2	Clump thickness	1–10	Tend to be grouped in monolayers	Often grouped in multiple layers
3	Uniformity of cell size	1–10	Evenly distributed	Unevenly distributed
4	Uniformity of cell shape	1–10	Evenly distributed	Unevenly distributed
5	Marginal adhesion	1–10	Tend to stick together	Tend not to stick together
6	Single epithelial cell size	1–10	Tend to be normal-sized	Tend to be significantly enlarged
7	Bare nuclei	1–10	Typically nuclei are not surrounded by cytoplasm of benign cells	Nuclei might be surrounded by cytoplasm
8	Bland chromatin	1–10	Uniform "texture" of nucleus	Coarser "texture" of nucleus
9	Normal nucleoli	1–10	Very small, if visible	More prominent, and greater in number
10	Mitoses	1–10	Grade of cancer determined by counting the number of mitoses (nuclear division, the process by which the cell divides and replicates)	
11	Class	2 or 4	2	4

Table 1. Attributes of Breast Cancer Wisconsin Data Set

The RENAME statement in the following DATA step enables you to assign a name to each variable so that you can understand it more easily:

```
data BreastCancer;
set BreastCancer;
rename var1=ID
       var2=Clump_Thickness
       var3=Uniformity_of_Cell_Size
       var4=Uniformity_of_Cell_Shape
       var5=Marginal_Adhesion
       var6=Single_Epithelial_Cell_Size
       var7=Bare_Nuclei
       var8=Bland_Chromatin
       var9=Normal_Nucleoli
       var10=Mitoses
       var11=Class;
run;
```

The following SAS program shows how you can use PROC HPBNET to analyze the BreastCancer data set:

```
proc hpbnet data=BreastCancer nbin=5 structure=Naive TAN PC MB bestmodel;
target Class;
id ID;
input Clump_Thickness Uniformity_of_Cell_Size  Uniformity_of_Cell_Shape
Marginal_Adhesion Single_Epithelial_Cell_Size Bare_Nuclei Bland_Chromatin
Normal_Nucleoli Mitoses/level=INT;
output network=net validinfo=vi varselect=vs
      varlevel=varl parameter=parm fit=fitstats pred=prediction;
partition fraction(validate=0.3 seed=12345);
code file="c:\hpbnetscorecode.sas" ;
run;
```

The TARGET statement specifies **Class** as the target variable. The ID statement specifies **ID** as the ID variable. The INPUT statement specifies that all the other variables are to be used as interval inputs. The NBIN= option in the PROC HPBNET statement specifies 5 for the number of equal-width bins for interval inputs. Four different structures are specified in the STRUCTURE= option (so each structure is trained), and the BESTMODEL option requests that PROC HPBNET automatically choose the best model to minimize the validation misclassification rate. The FRACTION option in the PARTITION statement requests that 30% of the data be used for validation (leaving 70% to be used for training). The OUTPUT statement specifies multiple output tables to be saved in the Work directory. The CODE statement specifies a filename (**hpbnetscorecode.sas**) where the generated score code is to be stored.

After you run PROC HPBNET, you can visualize the final model by using the **%createBNCdiagram** macro in the Appendix to view the selected Bayesian network structure. This macro takes the target variable and the output network data as arguments.

Figure 7 shows the generated diagram, which indicates that the naïve Bayes network is selected as the best structure for this data set, because the input variables are all conditionally independent of each other given the target.

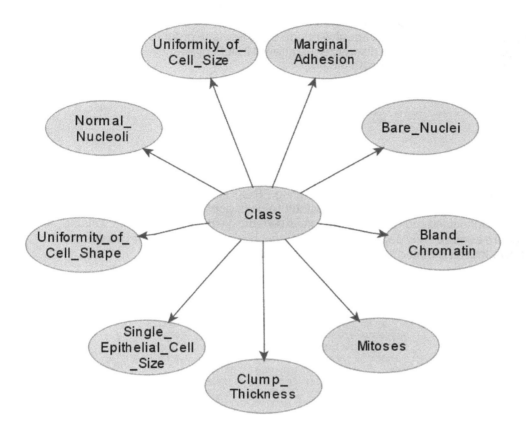

Figure 7. Bayesian Network Diagram

Table 2 through Table 7 show all the other output tables, which are stored in the Work directory.

The Best Model column in Table 2 shows that a naïve Bayesian network model with a maximum of one parent is selected, and the Misclassification Errors column shows that five validation observations are misclassified.

	Best Model	Misclassification Errors	Significance Threshold	Input Parameter: Prescreening	Input Parameter: Variable Selection	Input Parameter: Structure	Input Parameter: Parenting Method	Input Parameter: Maximum Number of Parents
1		5	0.05	1	1	PC	BESTSET	1
2		5	0.05	1	1	PC	BESTSET	2
3		5	0.05	1	1	PC	BESTSET	3
4		5	0.05	1	1	PC	BESTSET	4
5		5	0.05	1	1	PC	BESTSET	5
6		5	0.05	1	1	TAN	BESTSET	2
7	YES	5	0.05	1	1	NAIVE	BESTSET	1
8		5	0.05	1	1	NAIVE	BESTSET	2
9		5	0.05	1	1	NAIVE	BESTSET	3
10		5	0.05	1	1	NAIVE	BESTSET	4
11		5	0.05	1	1	NAIVE	BESTSET	5
12		44	0.05	1	3	MB	BESTSET	1
13		44	0.05	1	3	MB	BESTSET	2
14		44	0.05	1	3	MB	BESTSET	3
15		44	0.05	1	3	MB	BESTSET	4
16		44	0.05	1	3	MB	BESTSET	5

Table 2. Validation Information Table

Table 3 shows that the number of observations for validation is 178. Together with the misclassification errors shown in Table 2, you can calculate the validation accuracy as 1 − 5/178 = 97.19%. In PROC HPBNET, continuous variables are binned to equal-width discrete levels in order to simplify the model. If you want to improve this accuracy, you can discretize the interval inputs differently. For example, you could use entropy binning instead of equal-width binning.

	Number of Observations for Training	Number of Observations for Validation	Number of Observations Ignored	Sum of Frequencies for Training	Sum of Frequencies for Validation	Sum of Frequencies Ignored	Number of Nodes	Number of Links	Average Degree	Maximum Number of Parents in Network	Number of Parameters	Score
1	506	178	15	506	178	15	10	9	1.8	1	73	-4101.349933

Table 3. Fit Statistics Table

Table 4 shows the variable selection results. In the preceding PROC HPBNET call, the VARSELECT= option is not specified in the PROC statement, so its default value is applied. By default, each input variable is tested for conditional independence of the target variable given any other input variable, and only the variables that are conditionally dependent on the target given any other input variable are selected. Table 4 shows that all the nine input variables are selected into the model.

	Variable Name	Selected	Chi-Square Statistics	G-Square Statistics	P-Value of Chi-Square Statistics	P-Value of G-Square Statistics	Mutual Information	Degree of Freedom	Conditional Variables
1	Bare_Nuclei	YES	353.36783823	403.47623668	3.28698E-75	4.933826E-86	0.7412786201	4	
2	Bland_Chromatin	YES	300.12175361	354.16534484	1.019862E-63	2.211028E-75	0.7094932591	4	
3	Clump_Thickness	YES	288.29453088	335.88442772	3.626159E-61	1.955967E-71	0.696498837	4	
4	Marginal_Adhesion	YES	259.38424306	288.34682195	6.189801E-55	3.533217E-61	0.6590847963	4	
5	Mitoses	YES	110.78977073	115.6084875	4.93795E-23	4.62748E-24	0.4519447152	4	
6	Normal_Nucleoli	YES	315.99038507	349.49850642	3.845419E-67	2.250386E-74	0.7062430014	4	
7	Single_Epithelial_Cell_Size	YES	324.76623888	362.06155283	4.910373E-69	4.35991E-77	0.7148918452	4	
8	Uniformity_of_Cell_Shape	YES	381.82995416	458.83620861	2.343084E-81	5.339491E-98	0.772128209	4	
9	Uniformity_of_Cell_Size	YES	378.18381534	449.08950513	1.436784E-80	6.83417E-96	0.7670255046	4	

Table 4. Selected Variables Table

Table 5 shows the details for each level of the target and input variables. The values of 0–4 in the Level Index column indicate that PROC HPBNET bins each interval input variable into five equal-width levels The number of bins can be specified in the NBIN= option; by default, NBIN=5.

	Variable Name	Level Index		Level Value	Frequency
1	Class	0	4		178
2	Class	1	2		328
3	Bare_Nuclei	0	<2.8		323
4	Bare_Nuclei	1	<4.6		32
5	Bare_Nuclei	2	<6.4		21
6	Bare_Nuclei	3	<8.2		23
7	Bare_Nuclei	4	>=8.2		107
8	Bland_Chromatin	0	<2.8		230
9	Bland_Chromatin	1	<4.6		151
10	Bland_Chromatin	2	<6.4		35
11	Bland_Chromatin	3	<8.2		70
12	Bland_Chromatin	4	>=8.2		20
13	Clump_Thickness	0	<2.8		140
14	Clump_Thickness	1	<4.6		138
15	Clump_Thickness	2	<6.4		117
16	Clump_Thickness	3	<8.2		50
17	Clump_Thickness	4	>=8.2		61
18	Marginal_Adhesion	0	<2.8		341
19	Marginal_Adhesion	1	<4.6		62
20	Marginal_Adhesion	2	<6.4		34
21	Marginal_Adhesion	3	<8.2		28
22	Marginal_Adhesion	4	>=8.2		41
23	Mitoses	0	<2.8		442
24	Mitoses	1	<4.6		36
25	Mitoses	2	<6.4		5
26	Mitoses	3	<8.2		15
27	Mitoses	4	>=8.2		8
28	Normal_Nucleoli	0	<2.8		347
29	Normal_Nucleoli	1	<4.6		46
30	Normal_Nucleoli	2	<6.4		31
31	Normal_Nucleoli	3	<8.2		28
32	Normal_Nucleoli	4	>=8.2		54
33	Single_Epithelial_Cell_Size	0	<2.8		313
34	Single_Epithelial_Cell_Size	1	<4.6		86
35	Single_Epithelial_Cell_Size	2	<6.4		61
36	Single_Epithelial_Cell_Size	3	<8.2		24
37	Single_Epithelial_Cell_Size	4	>=8.2		22
38	Uniformity_of_Cell_Shape	0	<2.8		301
39	Uniformity_of_Cell_Shape	1	<4.6		72
40	Uniformity_of_Cell_Shape	2	<6.4		46
41	Uniformity_of_Cell_Shape	3	<8.2		43
42	Uniformity_of_Cell_Shape	4	>=8.2		44
43	Uniformity_of_Cell_Size	0	<2.8		310
44	Uniformity_of_Cell_Size	1	<4.6		70
45	Uniformity_of_Cell_Size	2	<6.4		42
46	Uniformity_of_Cell_Size	3	<8.2		34
47	Uniformity_of_Cell_Size	4	>=8.2		50

Table 5. Variable Levels Table

Table 6 shows the parameter values for the resulting model.

	Parameter Name	Parameter Value
1	ALPHA	0.05
2	PRESCREENING	1
3	VARSELECT	1
4	STRUCTURE	NAIVE
5	PARENTING	BESTSET
6	MAXPARENTS	1
7	MISSINGINT	IGNORE
8	MISSINGNOM	IGNORE
9	NBIN	5
10	INDEPTEST	CHIGSQUARE

Table 6. Parameter Table

Table 7 shows the prediction results for the first 20 observations of the training data. The Predicted: Class= columns contain the conditional probabilities for the **Class** variable, where Class=2 indicates a benign cell and Class=4 indicates a malignant cell. The conditional probabilities are then used to predict the target class. Here the target is known because these are the training data, but you can use this information to see how well the model is performing. The model is considered to perform well when the actual target class matches the target class that is predicted based on the conditional probabilities.

	ID	Class	Predicted: Class=4	Predicted: Class=2
1	1000025	2	0.0664101946	0.9335898054
2	1002945	2	0.9064857996	0.0935142004
3	1015425	2	0.0594603149	0.9405396851
4	1017122	4	0.9661046875	0.0338953125
5	1018561	2	0.05589358	0.94410642
6	1033078	2	0.053014663	0.946985337
7	1033078	2	0.0507343909	0.9492656091
8	1035283	2	0.05589358	0.94410642
9	1043999	2	0.0662214198	0.9337785802
10	1044572	4	0.9660008284	0.0339991716
11	1047630	4	0.9196798391	0.0803201609
12	1048672	2	0.0507343909	0.9492656091
13	1054593	4	0.9643091634	0.0356908366
14	1056784	2	0.0507343909	0.9492656091
15	1059552	2	0.05589358	0.94410642
16	1065726	4	0.7499639226	0.2500360774
17	1067444	2	0.048114632	0.951885368
18	1070935	2	0.0507343909	0.9492656091
19	1072179	4	0.9622871871	0.0377128129
20	1074610	2	0.05589358	0.94410642

Table 7. Prediction Results Table

PREDICTION ACCURACY COMPARISON

This section compares the prediction accuracy of Bayesian classifiers to that of their four popular competitor classifiers (decision tree, neural network, logistic regression, and support vector machines) for 25 data sets that were downloaded from the UCI Machine Learning Repository (Lichman 2013). Table 8 summarizes these data sets.

	Data Set	Attributes	Target Levels	Number of Observations	
				Total	Validation
1	Adult	13	2	48,842	16,116
2	Statlog (Australian Credit Approval)	14	2	690	CV-5
3	Breast Cancer Wisconsin (Original) (Mangasarian and Wolberg 1990)	9	2	699	CV-5
4	Car Evaluation	6	4	1,728	CV-5
5	Chess (King-Rook vs. King-Pawn)	36	2	3,196	1,066
6	Diabetes	8	2	768	CV-5
7	Solar Flare	10	2	1,066	CV-5
8	Statlog (German Credit Data)	24	2	1,000	CV-5
9	Glass Identification	9	6	214	CV-5
10	Heart Disease	13	2	270	CV-5
11	Hepatitis	19	2	155	CV-5
12	Iris	4	3	150	CV-5
13	LED Display Domain + 17 Irrelevant Attributes	24	10	3,190	1,057
14	Letter Recognition	16	26	20,000	4,937
15	Lymphography	18	4	148	CV-5
16	Nursery	8	5	12,960	4,319
17	Statlog (Landsat Satellite)	36	6	6,435	1,930
18	Statlog (Image Segmentation)	19	7	2,310	770
19	Soybean (Large)	35	19	683	CV-5
20	SPECT Heart	22	2	267	CV-5
21	Molecular Biology (Splice-Junction Gene Sequences)	60	3	3,190	1,053
22	Tic-Tac-Toe Endgame	9	2	958	CV-5
23	Statlog (Vehicle Silhouettes)	18	4	846	CV-5
24	Congressional Voting Records	16	2	435	CV-5
25	Waveform Database Generator (Version 1)	21	3	5,000	4,700

Table 8 Summary of 25 UCI Data Sets

For the larger data sets, the prediction accuracy was measured by the holdout method (that is, the learning process randomly selected two-thirds of the observations in the data set for building the classifiers, and then evaluated their prediction accuracy on the remaining observations in the data set). For smaller data sets, the prediction accuracy was measured by five-fold cross validation (CV-5). Each process was repeated five times. Observations that have missing values were removed from the data sets. All continuous variables in the data set were discretized with a tree-based binning method. The final average prediction accuracy values and their standard deviations are summarized in Table 9. The best accuracy values for each data set are marked in bold in each row of the table. You can see that PC and TAN in the five BN structures claim most of the wins and are competitive to the other classifiers.

Data Set	BN Classifiers					Competitor Classifiers			
	Naïve Bayes	BAN	TAN	PC	MB	Logistic	NN	Tree	SVM*
1 Adult	78.06+- 0.24	80.93+- 0.34	79.81+- 0.42	85.00+- 0.25	49.61+- 0.37	81.17+- 6.24	**85.84+- 0.27**	85.28+- 0.13	85.73+- 0.29
2 Statlog (Australian Credit Approval)	**86.43+- 0.33**	86.29+- 0.30	85.88+- 0.33	86.20+- 0.54	85.51+- 0.00	82.38+- 4.71	85.59+- 0.78	84.96+- 0.42	85.65+- 0.27
3 Breast Cancer Wisconsin (Original) (Mangasarian and Wolberg 1990)	**97.42+- 0.00**	**97.42+- 0.00**	96.65+- 0.39	97.17+- 0.12	96.88+- 0.40	95.82+- 0.57	96.54+- 0.45	94.11+- 0.40	96.42+- 0.20
4 Car Evaluation	80.01+- 0.21	86.56+- 1.03	87.52+- 0.10	88.24+- 0.90	86.52+- 1.27	77.26+- 0.26	93.07+- 0.49	**96.89+- 0.36**	
5 Chess (King-Rook vs. King-Pawn)	90.41+- 0.72	95.31+- 0.38	95.12+- 0.38	95.01+- 0.56	92.25+- 0.91	52.25+- 0.00	96.92+- 0.56	**99.04+- 0.39**	97.17+- 0.54
6 Diabetes	76.07+- 0.67	76.02+- 0.69	74.97+- 1.17	**78.10+- 0.70**	72.71+- 1.22	75.86+- 2.98	77.29+- 1.03	75.94+- 0.95	77.63+- 0.89
7 Solar Flare	73.58+- 0.79	73.94+- 0.92	73.60+- 0.78	80.02+-1.08	77.60+- 1.81	81.54+- 0.22	81.69+- 0.56	81.07+- 0.45	**82.18+- 0.42**
8 Statlog (German Credit Data)	71.60+- 0.55	71.28+- 1.02	71.94+- 1.29	**76.18+- 0.37**	66.40+- 1.47	75.24+- 0.50	75.04+- 0.34	72.18+- 0.59	75.86+- 0.76
9 Glass Identification	65.61+- 2.28	65.61+- 2.28	**71.68+- 1.02**	69.53+- 1.42	69.53+- 1.42	62.80+- 3.70	70.37+- 3.54	69.81+- 1.43	
10 Heart Disease	82.89+- 1.21	83.56+- 1.35	82.74+- 1.07	83.33+- 0.69	80.52+- 1.19	83.26+- 2.05	**84.67+- 1.30**	81.41+- 1.32	84.15+- 1.66
11 Hepatitis	86.60+- 1.86	86.61+- 1.20	88.73+- 2.60	90.56+- 1.34	92.11+- 1.94	88.69+- 3.25	91.59+- 1.85	**92.12+- 1.35**	91.06+- 1.22
12 Iris	**95.86+- 0.30**	**95.86+- 0.30**	95.19+- 0.74	**95.86+- 0.30**	**95.86+- 0.30**	80.37+- 0.72	94.92+- 1.40	94.53+- 0.86	
13 LED Display Domain + 17 Irrelevant Attributes	73.96+- 1.22	73.96+- 1.22	74.25+- 0.88	74.27+-1.17	**74.70+- 1.21**	19.79+- 0.73	73.25+- 0.39	74.08+- 0.92	
14 Letter Recognition	68.33+- 0.58	73.19+- 0.77	**78.75+- 0.63**	72.07+- 0.63	70.80+- 5.37	10.98+- 0.27	78.69+- 0.46	77.66+- 0.43	
15 Lymphography	80.81+- 1.56	81.49+- 1.83	79.32+- 0.77	**83.78+- 1.51**	74.19+- 3.71	61.62+- 3.89	81.35+- 1.56	74.86+- 0.88	
16 Nursery	82.92+- 0.65	86.46+- 0.69	89.25+- 0.39	91.45+- 0.63	91.02+- 0.25	90.86+- 0.34	92.27+- 0.47	**97.41+- 0.16**	
17 Statlog (Landsat Satellite)	81.39+- 0.73	86.36+- 0.51	86.31+- 0.79	86.58+- 0.49	84.56+- 0.65	72.78+- 0.29	**87.84+- 0.60**	85.55+- 0.38	
18 Statlog (Image Segmentation)	89.45+- 0.71	91.09+- 1.71	93.04+- 0.81	91.09+- 1.71	67.01+- 2.34	58.83+- 3.24	92.78+- 0.90	**93.56+- 0.74**	
19 Soybean (Large)	89.78+- 0.35	89.78+- 0.35	**92.97+- 0.99**	89.43+- 0.44	60.97+- 2.80	44.22+- 3.67	91.80+- 0.51	91.65+- 1.01	
20 SPECT Heart	72.06+- 1.65	75.36+- 1.04	73.41+- 1.38	80.60+- 1.25	69.96+- 2.74	78.35+- 1.66	**82.25+- 1.20**	79.33+- 1.51	81.95+- 1.97
21 Molecular Biology (Splice-Junction Gene Sequences)	95.31+- 0.51	95.38+- 0.47	95.71+- 0.71	**96.05+- 0.16**	92.61+- 7.13	80.46+- 1.61	95.48+- 0.70	94.17+- 0.62	
22 Tic-Tac-Toe Endgame	66.08+- 1.49	79.04+- 1.58	72.03+- 0.70	77.14+- 0.82	75.03+- 3.02	77.10+- 0.80	98.10+- 0.09	93.28+- 0.67	**98.33+- 0.00**
23 Statlog (Vehicle Silhouettes)	62.01+- 0.84	70.26+- 1.29	**71.25+- 0.80**	70.26+- 1.39	58.96+- 5.60	63.55+- 1.77	70.09+- 0.91	69.36+- 0.48	
24 Congressional Voting Records	94.80+- 0.53	95.17+- 0.16	95.13+- 0.72	94.90+- 0.10	94.99+- 0.38	93.79+- 2.11	**95.82+- 0.99**	95.08+- 0.42	95.40+- 0.43
25 Waveform Database Generator(Version 1)	78.31+- 1.48	78.31+- 1.48	73.68+- 1.77	78.35+- 1.33	78.62+- 1.50	62.43+- 3.43	**81.78+- 0.85**	70.27+- 3.06	

*SVM for binary target only

Table 9. Classification Accuracy on 25 UCI Machine Learning Data Sets

CONCLUSION

This paper describes Bayesian network (BN) classifiers, introduces the HPBNET procedure, and shows how you can use the procedure to build BN classifiers. It also compares the competitive prediction power of BN classifiers with other state-of-the-art classifiers, and shows how you can use a SAS macro to visualize the network structures.

REFERENCES

Lichman, M. 2013. "UCI Machine Learning Repository." School of Information and Computer Sciences, University of California, Irvine. http://archive.ics.uci.edu/ml.

Russell, S., and Norvig, P. 2010. *Artificial Intelligence: A Modern Approach*, 3rd ed. Upper Saddle River, New Jersey: Pearson.

Mangasarian, O. L., and Wolberg, W. H. 1990. "Cancer Diagnosis via Linear Programming", *SIAM News*, 23 (September): 1, 18.

ACKNOWLEDGMENTS

The authors would like to thank Yongqiao Xiao for reviewing this paper and Anne Baxter for editing it.

The breast cancer database was obtained from the University of Wisconsin Hospitals, Madison from Dr. William H. Wolberg.

The lymphography domain was obtained from the University Medical Centre, Institute of Oncology, Ljubljana, Yugoslavia. Thanks go to M. Zwitter and M. Soklic for providing the data.

The Vehicle Silhouettes data set comes from the Turing Institute, Glasgow, Scotland.

The creators of heart disease data set are:

1. Hungarian Institute of Cardiology. Budapest: Andras Janosi, M.D.

2. University Hospital, Zurich, Switzerland: William Steinbrunn, M.D.

3. University Hospital, Basel, Switzerland: Matthias Pfisterer, M.D.

4. V.A. Medical Center, Long Beach and Cleveland Clinic Foundation: Robert Detrano, M.D., Ph.D.

CONTACT INFORMATION

Your comments and questions are valued and encouraged. Contact the author at:

Ye Liu
ye.liu@sas.com

Weihua Shi
weihua.shi@sas.com

Wendy Czika
wendy.czika@sas.com

APPENDIX

```
%macro createBNCdiagram(target=Class, outnetwork=net);

   data outstruct;
       set &outnetwork;
       if strip(upcase(_TYPE_)) eq 'STRUCTURE' then output;
       keep _nodeid_  _childnode_ _parentnode_;
   run;

   data networklink;
      set outstruct;
      linkid = _N_;
      label linkid ="Link ID";
   run;

   proc sql;
      create table work._node1 as
         select distinct _CHILDNODE_ as  node
         from networklink;
      create table work._node2  as
         select distinct _PARENTNODE_  as node
         from networklink;
   quit;

   proc sql;
      create table work._node as
         select node
         from work._node1
         UNION
         select node
         from work._node2;
   quit;

   data bnc_networknode;
      length NodeType $32.;
      set work._node;
      if strip(upcase(node)) eq strip(upcase("&target")) then do;
        NodeType = "TARGET";
        NodeColor=2;
      end;
      else  do;
        NodeType = "INPUT";
        NodeColor = 1;
      end;
      label NodeType ="Node Type" ;
      label NodeColor ="Node Color" ;

   run;

   data parents(rename=(_parentnode_ = _node_)) children(rename=(_childnode_
= _node_)) links;
      length _parentnode_ _childnode_ $ 32;
      set networklink;
      keep _parentnode_ _childnode_ ;
   run;
```

17

```
    /*get list of all unique nodes*/
    data nodes;
        set parents children;
    run;

    proc sort data=nodes;
        by _node_;
    run;

    data nodes;
        set nodes;
        by _node_;
        if first._node_;
        _Parentnode_ = _node_;
        _childnode_ = "";
    run;

    /*merge node color and type */
    data nodes;
        merge nodes bnc_
 networknode (rename=(node=_node_ nodeColor=_nodeColor_
nodeType=_nodeType_));
        by _node_;
    run;

    /*sort color values to ensure consistent color mapping across networks */
    /*note that the color mapping is HTML style dependent though */
    proc sort data=nodes;
        by _nodeType_;
    run;

    /*combine nodes and links*/
    /* need outsummaryall for model report*/
    data bnc_networksummary(drop=_shape_ _nodecolor_ _nodepriority_ _shape_
_nodeID_ _nodetype_ _linkdirection_) bnc_networksummaryall;
        length _parentnode_ _childnode_ $ 32;
        set nodes links;
        drop _node_;
        if _childnode_ EQ "" thendo;
                _nodeID_ = _parentnode_;
                _nodepriority_ = 1;
                _shape_= "OVAL";
            end;
        else do;
          _linkdirection_ = "TO";
          output bnc_networksummary;
        end;
        output bnc_networksummaryall;
        label _linkdirection_="Link Direction";
    run;

     proc datasets lib=work nolist nowarn;
        delete _node _node1 _node2 nodes links parents children;
    run;

    quit;
```

```
proc template;
    define statgraph bpath;
        begingraph / DesignHeight=720 DesignWidth=720;
            entrytitle "Bayesian Network Diagram";
            layout region;
                pathdiagram fromid=_parentnode_ toid=_childnode_ /
                arrangement=GRIP
                nodeid=_nodeid_
                nodelabel=_nodeID_
                nodeshape=_shape_
                nodepriority=_nodepriority_
                linkdirection=_linkdirection_
                nodeColorGroup=_NodeColor_
                          textSizeMin = 10
                ;
            endlayout;
        endgraph;
    end;
run;

ods graphics;
proc sgrender data=bnc_networksummaryall template=bpath;
run;

%mend;

%createBNCdiagram;
```

Stacked Ensemble Models for Improved Prediction Accuracy

Funda Güneş, Russ Wolfinger, and Pei-Yi Tan

SAS Institute Inc.

ABSTRACT

Ensemble modeling is now a well-established means for improving prediction accuracy; it enables you to average out noise from diverse models and thereby enhance the generalizable signal. Basic stacked ensemble techniques combine predictions from multiple machine learning algorithms and use these predictions as inputs to second-level learning models. This paper shows how you can generate a diverse set of models by various methods such as forest, gradient boosted decision trees, factorization machines, and logistic regression and then combine them with stacked-ensemble techniques such as hill climbing, gradient boosting, and nonnegative least squares in SAS® Visual Data Mining and Machine Learning. The application of these techniques to real-world big data problems demonstrates how using stacked ensembles produces greater prediction accuracy and robustness than do individual models. The approach is powerful and compelling enough to alter your initial data mining mindset from finding the single best model to finding a collection of really good complementary models. It does involve additional cost due both to training a large number of models and the proper use of cross validation to avoid overfitting. This paper shows how to efficiently handle this computational expense in a modern SAS® environment and how to manage an ensemble workflow by using parallel computation in a distributed framework.

INTRODUCTION

Ensemble methods are commonly used to boost predictive accuracy by combining the predictions of multiple machine learning models. Model stacking is an efficient ensemble method in which the predictions that are generated by using different learning algorithms are used as inputs in a second-level learning algorithm. This second-level algorithm is trained to optimally combine the model predictions to form a final set of predictions (Sill et al. 2009).

In the last decade, model stacking has been successfully used on a wide variety of predictive modeling problems to boost the models' prediction accuracy beyond the level obtained by any of the individual models. This is sometimes referred to as a "wisdom of crowds" approach, pulling from the age-old philosophy of Aristotle. Ensemble modeling and model stacking are especially popular in data science competitions, in which a sponsor posts training and test data and issues a global challenge to produce the best model for a specified performance criterion. The winning model is almost always an ensemble model. Often individual teams develop their own ensemble model in the early stages of the competition and then join forces in the later stages. One such popular site is Kaggle, and you are encouraged to explore numerous winning solutions that are posted in the discussion forums there to get a flavor of the state of the art.

The diversity of the models in a library plays a key role in building a powerful ensemble model. Dieterich (2000) emphasizes the importance of diversity by stating, "A necessary and sufficient condition for an ensemble model to be more accurate than any of its individual members is if the classifiers are accurate and diverse." By combining information from diverse modeling approaches, ensemble models gain more accuracy and robustness than a fine-tuned single model can gain. There are many parallels with successful human teams in business, science, politics, and sports, in which each team member makes a significant contribution and individual weaknesses and biases are offset by the strengths of other members.

Overfitting is an omnipresent concern in ensemble modeling because a model library includes so many models that predict the same target. As the number of models in a model library increases, the chances of building overfitting ensemble models increases greatly. A related problem is leakage, in which

1

information from the target inadvertently and sometimes surreptitiously works its way into the model-checking mechanism and causes an overly optimistic assessment of generalization performance. The most efficient techniques that practitioners commonly use to minimize overfitting and leakage include cross validation, regularization, and bagging. This paper covers applications of these techniques for building ensemble models that can generalize well to new data.

This paper first provides an introduction to SAS Visual Data Mining and Machine Learning in SAS® Viya™, which is a new single, integrated, in-memory environment. The section following that discusses how to generate a diverse library of machine learning models for stacking while avoiding overfitting and leakage, and then shows an approach to building a diverse model library for a binary classification problem. A subsequent section shows how to perform model stacking by using regularized regression models, including nonnegative least squares regression. Another section demonstrates stacking with the scalable gradient boosting algorithm and focuses on an automatic tuning implementation that is based on efficient distributed and parallel paradigms for training and tuning models in the SAS Viya platform. The penultimate section shows how to build powerful ensemble models with the hill climbing technique. The last section compares the stacked ensemble models that are built by each approach to a naïve ensemble model and the single best model, and also provides a brief summary.

OVERVIEW OF THE SAS VIYA ENVIRONMENT

The SAS programs used in this paper are built in the new SAS Viya environment. SAS Viya uses SAS® Cloud Analytic Services (CAS) to perform tasks and enables you to build various model scenarios in a consistent environment, resulting in improved productivity, stability, and maintainability. SAS Viya represents a major rearchitecture of core data processing and analytical components in SAS software to enable computations across a large distributed grid in which it is typically more efficient to move algorithmic code rather than to move data.

The smallest unit of work for the CAS server is a CAS action. CAS actions can load data, transform data, compute statistics, perform analytics, and create output. Each action is configured by specifying a set of input parameters. Running a CAS action in the CAS server processes the action's parameters and the data to create an action result.

In SAS Viya, you can run CAS actions via a variety of interfaces, including the following:

- SAS session, which uses the CAS procedure. PROC CAS uses the CAS language (CASL) for specifying CAS actions and their input parameters. The CAS language also supports normal program logic such as conditional and looping statements and user-written functions.

- Python or Lua, which use the SAS Scripting Wrapper for Analytics Transfer (SWAT) libraries

- Java, which uses the CAS Client class

- Representational state transfer (REST), which uses the CAS REST APIs

CAS actions are organized into action sets, where each action set defines an application programming interface (API). SAS Viya currently provides the following action sets:

- Data mining and machine learning action sets support gradient boosted trees, neural networks, factorization machines, support vector machines, graph and network analysis, text mining, and more.

- Statistics action sets compute summary statistics and perform clustering, regression, sampling, principal component analysis, and more.

- Analytics action sets provide additional numeric and text analytics.

- System action sets run SAS code via the DATA step or DS2, manage CAS libraries and tables, manage CAS servers and sessions, and more.

SAS Viya also provides CAS-powered procedures, which enable you to have the familiar experience of coding traditional SAS procedures. Behind each statement in these procedures is one or more CAS actions that run across multiple machines. The SAS Viya platform enables you to program with both CAS actions and procedures, providing you with maximum flexibility to build an optimal ensemble.

SAS Visual Data Mining and Machine Learning integrates CAS actions and CAS-powered procedures and surfaces in-memory machine-learning techniques such as gradient boosting, factorization machines, neural networks, and much more through its interactive visual interface, SAS® Studio tasks, procedures, and a Python client. This product bundle is an industry-leading platform for analyzing complex data, building predictive models, and conducting advanced statistical operations (Wexler, Haller, and Myneni 2017).

For more information about SAS Viya and SAS Visual Data Mining and Machine Learning, see the section "Recommended Reading." For specific code examples from this paper, refer to the Github repository referenced in that section.

BUILDING A STRONG LIBRARY OF DIVERSE MODELS

You can generate a diverse set of models by using many different machine learning algorithms at various hyperparameter settings. Forest and gradient bosting methods are themselves based on the idea of combining diverse decision tree models. The forest method generates diverse models by training decision trees on a number of bootstrap samples of the training set, whereas the gradient boosting method generates a diverse set of models by fitting models to sequentially adjusted residuals, a form of stochastic gradient descent. In a broad sense, even multiple regression models can be considered to be an ensemble of single regression models, with weights determined by least squares. Whereas the traditional wisdom in the literature is to combine so-called "weak" learners, the modern approach is to create an ensemble of a well-chosen collection of strong yet diverse models.

In addition to using many different modeling algorithms, the diversity in a model library can be further enhanced by randomly subsetting the rows (observations) and/or columns (features) in the training set. Subsetting rows can be done with replacement (bootstrap) or without replacement (for example, k-fold cross validation). The word "bagging" is often used loosely to describe such subsetting; it can also be used to describe subsetting of columns. Columns can be subsetted randomly or in a more principled fashion that is based on some computed measure of importance. The variety of choices for subsetting columns opens the door to the large and difficult problem of feature selection.

Each new big data set tends to bring its own challenges and intricacies, and no single fixed machine learning algorithm is known to dominate. Furthermore, each of the main classes of algorithms has a set of hyperparameters that must be specified, leading to an effectively infinite set of possible models you can fit. In order to navigate through this model space and achieve near optimal performance for a machine learning task, a basic brute-force strategy is to first build a reasonably large collection of model fits across a well-designed grid of settings and then compare, reduce, and combine them in some intelligent fashion. A modern distributed computing framework such as SAS Viya makes this strategy quite feasible.

AVOIDING LEAKAGE WHILE STACKING

A naïve ensembling approach is to directly take the predictions of the test data from a set of models that are fit on the full training set and use them as inputs to a second-level model, say a simple regression model. This approach is almost guaranteed to overfit the data because the target responses have been used twice, a form of data leakage. The resulting model almost always generalizes poorly for a new data set that has previously unseen targets. The following subsections describe the most common techniques for combatting leakage and selecting ensembles that will perform well on future data.

SINGLE HOLDOUT VALIDATION SET

The classic way to avoid overfitting is to set aside a fraction of the training data and treat its target labels as unseen until final evaluation of a model fitting process. This approach has been the main one available in SAS Enterprise Miner from its inception, and it remains a simple and reliable way to assess model accuracy. It can be the most efficient way to compare models. It also is the way most data science competitions are structured for data sets that have a large number of rows.

For stacked ensembling, this approach also provides a good way to assess ensembles that are made on the dedicated training data. However, it provides no direct help in constructing those ensembles, nor does it provide any measure of variability in the model performance metric because you obtain only a single number. The latter concern can be addressed by scoring a set of bootstrap or other well-chosen random samples of the single holdout set.

K-FOLD CROSS VALIDATION AND OUT-OF-FOLD PREDICTIONS

The main idea of cross validation is to repeat the single holdout concept across different folds of the data—that is, to sequentially train a model on one part of the data and then observe the behavior of this trained model on the other held-out part, for which you know the ground truth. Doing so enables you to simulate performance on previously unseen targets and aims to decrease the bias of the learners with respect to the training data.

Assuming that each observation has equal weight, it makes sense to hold out each with equal frequency. The original jackknife (leave-one-out cross validation) method in regression holds out one observation at a time, but this method tends to be computationally infeasible for more complex algorithms and large data sets. A better approach is to hold out a significant fraction of the data (typically 10 or 20%) and divide the training data into k folds, where k is 5 or 10. The following simple steps are used to obtain five-fold cross validated predictions:

1. Divide the training data into five disjoint folds of as nearly equal size as possible, and possibly also stratify by target frequencies or means.

2. Hold out each fold one at a time.

3. Train the model on the remaining data.

4. Assess the trained model by using the holdout set.

Fitting and scoring for all k versions of the training and holdout sets provides holdout (cross validated) predictions for each of the samples in your original training data. These are known as out-of-fold (OOF) predictions. The sum of squared errors between the OOF predictions and true target values yields the cross validation error of a model, and is typically a good measure of generalizability. Furthermore, the OOF predictions are usually safely used as inputs for second-level stacked ensembling.

You might be able to further increase the robustness of your OOF predictions by repeating the entire k-fold exercise, recomputing OOFs with different random folds, and averaging the results. However, you must be careful to avoid possible subtle leakage if too many repetitions are done. Determining the best number of repetitions is not trivial. You can determine the best number by doing nested k-fold cross validation, in which you perform two-levels of k-fold cross validation (one within the other) and assess performance at the outer level. In this nested framework, the idea is to evaluate a small grid of repetition numbers, determine which one performs best, and then use this number for subsequent regular k-fold evaluations. You can also use this approach to help choose k if you suspect that the common values of 5 or 10 are suboptimal for your data.

Cross validation can be used both for tuning hyperparameters and for evaluating model performance. When you use the same data both for tuning and for estimating the generalization error with k-fold cross validation, you might have information leakage and the resulting model might overfit the data. To deal with this overfitting problem, you can use nested k-fold cross validation—you use the inner loop for parameter tuning, and you use the outer loop to estimate the generalization error (Cawley and Talbot 2010).

BAGGING AND OUT-OF-BAG PREDICTIONS

A technique similar in spirit to k-fold cross-validation is classical bagging, in which numerous bootstrap samples (with replacement) are constructed and the out-of-bag (OOB) predictions are used to assess model performance. One potential downside to this approach is the uneven number of times each observation is held out and the potential for some missing values. However, this downside is usually inconsequential if you perform an appropriate number of bootstrap repetitions (for example, 100). This type of operation is very suitable for parallel processing, where with the right framework generating 100 bootstrap samples will not take much more clock time than 10 seconds.

AN APPROACH TO BUILDING A STRONG, DIVERSE MODEL LIBRARY

EXAMPLE: ADULT SALARY DATA SET

This section describes how to build a strong and diverse model library by using the Adult data set from the UCI Machine Learning Repository (Lichman 2013). This data set has 32,561 training samples and16,281 test samples; it includes 13 input variables, which are a mix of nominal and interval variables that include education, race, marital status, capital gain, and capital loss. The target is a binary variable that takes a value of 1 if a person makes less than 50,000 a year and value of 0 otherwise. The training and test set are available in a GitHub repository, for which a link is provided in the section "Recommended Reading."

Treating Nominal Variables

The data set includes six nominal variables that have various levels. The cardinality of the categorical variables is reduced by collapsing the rare categories and making sure that each distinct level has at least 2% of the samples. For example, the cardinality of the work class variable is reduced from 8 to 7, and the cardinality of the occupation variable is reduced from 14 to 12.

The nominal variable *education* is dropped from the analysis, because the corresponding interval variable (*education_num*) already exists. All the remaining nominal variables are converted to numerical variables by using likelihood encoding as described in the next section.

Likelihood Encoding and Feature Engineering

Likelihood encoding involves judiciously using the target variable to create numeric versions of categorical features. The most common way of doing this is to replace each level of the categorical variable with the mean of the target over all observations that have that level. Doing this carries a danger of information leakage that might result in significant overfitting. The best way to combat the danger of leakage is to perform the encoding separately for each distinct version of the training data during cross validation. For example, while doing five-fold cross validation, you compute the likelihood-encoded categorical variable anew for each of the five training sets and use these values in the corresponding holdout sets. A drawback of this approach is the extra calculations and bookkeeping that are required.

If the cardinality of a categorical variable is small relative to the number of observations and if the binary target is not rare, it can be acceptable to do the likelihood encoding once up front and run the risk of a small amount of leakage. For the sake of illustration and convenience, that approach is taken here with the Adult data set, because the maximum cardinality of the nominal variables is 12.

Likelihood encoding has direct ties to classical statistical methods such as one-way ANOVA, and it can be viewed as stacking the simple predictions from such models. More sophisticated versions involve shrinking the encoded means toward an overall mean, which can be particularly effective when the class sizes are imbalanced. This approach is well-known to improve mean square prediction error and is popularly known as L2 regularization in machine learning communities and as ridge regression or best linear unbiased prediction (BLUP) in statistical communities. Alternatively, you can use an L1 (LASSO) norm and shrink toward the median. Note also that likelihood encoding effectively performs the same operation that tree-based methods perform at their first step—that is, sorting categories by their target likelihood in order to find the best way to split them into two groups.

5

Stacking and Building the Model Library

As an illustrative small example, you can use the following three-level stacked ensemble approach along with four different machine learning algorithms (gradient boosting, forest, factorization machines, and logistic regression):

Level 1: Fit initial models and find good hyperparameters using cross validation and automatic tuning (also called autotuning).

Level 2: Create 100 bootstrap samples of the training set, and subsequently divide each of these samples into five folds. For each individual training set, train the four models (by using five-fold cross validation) and create 100 sets of five-fold OOF predictions. This approach effectively creates 400 total OOF predictions with approximately 1/3 of the values missing because of the properties of bootstrap (with replacement) sampling.

Level 3: Average together the nonmissing OOF predictions for each learning algorithm, creating four total average OOF predictions (one for each learning algorithm). Use LASSO, nonnegative least squares, gradient boosting, and hill climbing on these four features to obtain the final predictions.

As you move through the levels, you also create features on the final testing data. It is usually wise to keep training and testing features close to each other while coding. Otherwise you increase the risk of making a mistake at testing time because of an oversight in indexing or scoring. This practice also helps you keep your final goal in mind and ensure that everything you are doing is applicable to unlabeled testing rows.

Results for Level 1

Level 1 creates an initial small diverse library of models by using gradient boosting, forest, factorization machines, and logistic regression on the SAS Viya platform, which trains and tunes models quickly via in-memory processing by taking advantage of both multithreading and distributed computing. These algorithms include a fair number of hyperparameters that must be specified, and a manual tuning process can be difficult. Instead, you can use the efficient random search capability in the AUTOTUNE statement available in the GRADBOOST (scalable gradient boosting), FOREST, and the FACTMAC (factorization machines) procedures. By using autotuning, you can rapidly reduce the model error that is produced by default settings of these hyperparameters. This automated search provides an efficient search path through the hyperparameter space by taking advantage of parallel computing in the SAS Viya platform. The AUTOTUNE statement is also available in the NNET (neural network), TREESPLIT (decision tree), and SVMACHINE (support vector machine) procedures of SAS Viya Data Mining and Machine Learning. You can see an example of how autotuning is used in the section "Stacking with the Scalable Gradient Boosting Algorithm." You must be wary of overfitting and leakage while doing this tuning. For more information about automated search, see Koch et al. (2017).

Results for Level 2

After finding good set of hyperparameter values for each of the four modeling algorithms, Level 2 generates 100 bootstrap replications (sampling with replacement) of the training data. Each training set is then divided into five disjoint folds, which produces five versions of new training sets (each version omits one fold) for each of the bootstrap samples. Notice that this setup produces 500 (100 x 5) versions of training sets. Forest, gradient boosting, factorization machine, and logistic regression models are trained on each of these training sets and the left-out folds are scored. In total, 2,000 (500 x 4) models are trained and scored. For each bootstrap sample, the five sets of OOF predictions are combined, which produces 400 columns of five-fold OOF predictions (100 gradient boosting, 100 forest, 100 logistic models, and 100 factorization machines).

Because bootstrap sampling uses sampling with replacement, it results in some missing predictions in addition to multiple predictions for the same IDs. This example adopts the following approach to deal with these issues and arrive at one prediction for each ID:

- If an ID is selected more than once, the average prediction is used for each ID.

- After making sure that each ID is selected at least once in the 100 bootstrap samples of each modeling algorithm, mean OOF predictions are obtained by averaging over 100 bootstrap OOF predictions. This simple averaging provided a significant reduction in the five-fold training ASE. For example, for the gradient boosting model, the five-fold training ASE of the best model (out of 100 models) was 0.09351. When the OOF predictions of 100 gradient boosting models are averaged, this value reduced to 0.09236.

This approach produces four columns of OOF predictions (one for each of the four algorithms). These four averaged models form the model library to be used in Level-3 stacking.

For scoring on test data, the predictions from the 500 models, which are generated by the same learning algorithm, are simply averaged.

Figure 1 shows the five-fold cross validation and test average squared errors (ASEs, also often called mean squared error, or MSE) of the four average models that form the model library to be used in Level-3 stacking. The best performing single modeling method is the average gradient boosting model, which has a five-fold cross validation ASE of 0.09236. It is best by a fairly significant margin according to the ASE performance metric.

Level-2 Models	Training ASE (Five-Fold CV ASE)	Testing ASE
Average gradient boosting	0.09236	0.09273
Average forest	0.09662	0.09665
Average logistic regression	0.10470	0.10370
Average factorization machines	0.11160	0.10930

Figure 1. Five-Fold Cross Validation and Test ASEs of Models in the Model Library

Results for Level 3

With average OOF predictions in hand from Level 2, you are ready to build final ensembles and assess the resulting models by using the test set predictions. The OOF predictions are stored in the SAS data set train_mean_oofs, which includes four columns of OOF predictions for the four average models, an ID variable, and the target variable. The corresponding test set is test_mean_preds which includes the same columns. The rest of the analyses in this paper use these two data sets, which are also available in the GitHub repository.

Start a CAS Session and Load Data into CAS

The following SAS code starts a CAS session and loads data into in the CAS in-memory distributed computing engine in the SAS Viya environment:

```
/* Start a CAS session named mySession */
cas mySession;

/* Define a CAS engine libref for CAS in-memory data tables  */
/* Define a SAS libref for the directory that includes the data */
libname cas sasioca;
libname data "/folders/myfolders/";

/* Load data into CAS using SAS DATA steps */
data cas.train_oofs;
  set data.train_mean_oofs;
run;
data cas.test_preds;
  set data.test_mean_preds;
run;
```

REGRESSION STACKING

Let Y represent the target, X represent the space of inputs, and $g_1, \dots, g_L$ denote the learned predictions from L machine learning algorithms (for example, a set of out-of-fold predictions). For an interval target, a linear ensemble model builds a prediction function,

$$b(g) = w_1 * g_1 + \cdots + w_L * g_L$$

where w_i are the model weights. A simple way to specify these weights is to set them all equal to $1/_L$ (as done in Level-2) so that each model contributes equally to the final ensemble. You can alternatively assign higher weight to models you think will perform better. For the Adult example, the gradient boosted tree OOF predictor is a natural candidate to weight higher because of its best single model performance.

Although assigning weights by hand can often be reasonable, you can typically improve final ensemble performance by using a learning algorithm to estimate them. Because of its computational efficiency and model interpretability, linear regression is a commonly used method for final model stacking. In a regression model that has an interval target, the model weights (w_i) are found by solving the following least squares problem:

$$min \sum_{i=1}^{N} (y_i - (w_1 * g_{1i} + \cdots + w_L * g_{Li}))^2$$

REGULARIZATION

Using cross validated predictions partially helps to deal with the overfitting problem. An attending difficulty with using OOF or OOB predictions as inputs is that they tend to be highly correlated with each other, creating the well-known collinearity problem for regression fitting. Arguably the best way to deal with this problem is to use some form of regularization for the model weights when training the highest-level model. Regularization methods place one or more penalties on the objective function, based on the size of the model weights. If these penalty parameters are selected correctly, the total prediction error of the model can decrease significantly and the parameters of the resulting model can be more stable.

The following subsections illustrate a couple of good ways to regularize your ensemble model. They involve estimating and choosing one or more new hyperparameters that control the amount of regularization. These hyperparameters can be determined by various methods, including a single validation data partition, cross validation, and information criteria.

Stacking with Adaptive LASSO

Consider a linear regression of the following form:

$$b(x) = w_1 * g_1 + \cdots + w_L * g_L$$

A LASSO learner finds the model weights by placing an L_1 (sum of the absolute value of the weights) penalty on the model weights as follows:

$$min \sum_{i=1}^{N} (y_i - (w_1 * g_{1i} + \cdots + w_L * g_{Li}))^2$$

$$\text{subject to} \sum_{i=1}^{L} |w_i| \leq t$$

If the LASSO hyperparameter *t* is small enough, some of the weights will be exactly 0. Thus, the LASSO method produces a sparser and potentially more interpretable model. Adaptive LASSO (Zou 2006) modifies the LASSO penalty by applying adaptive weights (v_j) to each parameter that forms the LASSO constraint:

$$\text{subject to } \sum_{i=1}^{L} (v_i |w_i|) \leq t$$

These constraints control shrinking the zero coefficients more than they control shrinking the nonzero coefficients.

The following REGSELECT procedure run builds an adaptive LASSO model. By default, the procedure uses the inverse of the full linear regression model coefficients for v_j (Güneş 2015).

```
proc regselect data=cas.train_mean_oofs;
    partition fraction(validate=0.3);
    model target = mean_factmac mean_gbt mean_logit mean_frst / noint;
    selection method=lasso
        (adaptive stop=sbc choose=validate) details=steps;
    code file="/c/output/lasso_score.sas";
run;
```

The PARTITION statement reserves 30% of the data for validation, leaving the remaining 70% for training. The validation part of the data is used to find the optimal value for the adaptive LASSO parameter *t*. The MODEL statement specifies the four average OOF predictions from Level 2 as input variables. The SELECTION statement requests the adaptive LASSO method, and the CHOOSE=VALIDATE suboption requests that the selected regularization parameter (*t*) be used to minimize the validation error on the 30% single holdout set. The CODE statement saves the resulting scoring code in the specified directory.

Figure 2 shows the results. The gradient boosted predictor receives around 94% of the weight in the resulting ensemble, with the remaining 6% going to the forest model, along with just a little contribution from factorization machines. The ASE appears to have improved a little, but keep in mind that these results are on a new 30% holdout.

Parameter Estimates		
Parameter	DF	Estimate
mean_factmac	1	0.001931
mean_gbt	1	0.938671
mean_frst	1	0.058570

ASE (Train)	0.09214
ASE (Validate)	0.09263

Figure 2. Parameter Estimates and Fit statistics for the Adaptive LASSO Stacking Model

To obtain a better measure of prediction error, you can check the ASE of the resulting model for the test set. The following SAS statements first score for the test set by using the saved score code, lasso_score.sas, and then calculate the ASE:

```
data cas.lasso_score;
    set cas.test_preds;
    %include '/c/output/lasso_score.sas';
run;

data cas.lasso_score;
    se=(p_target-target)*(p_target-target);
run;

proc cas;
    summary/ table={name='lasso_score', vars={'se'}};
run;
quit;
```

The **summary** CAS action outputs the test ASE of the adaptive LASSO ensemble model as 0.09269, which improves slightly on the average gradient boosting model, whose test ASE is 0.09273.

Stacking with Nonnegative Weights Regularization

Another regularization technique that is commonly used to build a stacked regression model is to restrict the regression coefficients to be nonnegative while performing regression. Breiman (1995) shows that when the regression coefficients are constrained to be nonnegative, the resulting ensemble models exhibit better prediction error than any of the individual models in the library. Because each model takes a nonnegative weight, the resulting ensemble model can also be interpreted more easily. The paper also shows that the additional commonly used restriction $\Sigma\, w_i = 1$ does not further improve the prediction accuracy, which is consistent with the findings here for the Adult data. A linear regression model that places nonnegative weights on a squared error loss function has the following form:

$$\min \sum_{i=1}^{N} (y_i - (w_1 * g_{1i} + \cdots + w_L * g_{Li}))^2$$

$$\text{subject to } w_i > 0, \qquad \text{for i} = 1, \dots, L$$

The following CQLIM procedure statements from SAS® Econometrics fit a linear least squares regression model with nonnegativity constraints on the regression weights:

```
proc cqlim data=cas.train_mean_oofs;
    model target= mean_gbt mean_frst mean_logit mean_factmac;
    restrict mean_gbt>0;
    restrict mean_frst>0;
    restrict mean_logit>0;
    restrict mean_factmac>0;
    output out=cas.cqlim_preds xbeta copyvar=target;
    ods output ParameterEstimates=paramests;
run;
```

Figure 3 shows the "Parameter Estimates" table that is generated by the CQLIM procedure. The Estimate column shows the regression weights of the stacked nonnegative least squares model for each of the four models. Here factorization machines have a slightly larger weight than in the previous adaptive LASSO model.

Parameter Estimates					
Parameter	DF	Estimate	Standard Error	t Value	Approx Pr > |t|
mean_gbt	1	0.921430	0.024091	38.25	<.0001
mean_factmac	1	0.022345	0.012701	1.76	0.0785
mean_frst	1	0.056071	0.025714	2.18	0.0292
mean_logit	1	1.0536712E-8	0	.	.

Figure 3. Regression Weights for the Nonnegative Least Squares Stacking Model

This stacked model produces a training error of 0.09228 and a testing error of 0.09269, which provides an improvement over the single best Level-2 model: the average gradient boosting model, which has a training ASE of 0.09236 and a testing ASE of 0.09273.

STACKING WITH THE SCALABLE GRADIENT BOOSTING ALGORITHM AND AUTOTUNING

Model stacking is not limited to basic models such as linear regression; any supervised learning algorithm can be used as a higher-level learning algorithm as long as it helps boost the prediction accuracy. In fact, nonlinear algorithms such as boosted trees and neural networks have been successfully used as a second- and third-level modeling algorithms in winning methods of various data science competitions.

The GRADBOOST procedure in SAS Visual Data Mining and Machine Learning fits a scalable gradient boosting model that is based that is on the boosting method described in Hastie, Tibshirani, and Friedman (2001), and its functionality is comparable to the popular **xgboost** program. PROC GRADBOOST is computationally efficient and uses fewer resources than the Gradient Boosting node in SAS Enterprise Miner uses.

The following GRADBOOST procedure run trains a stacked ensemble model by using the Level-2 OOF predictions of the four average models:

```
proc gradboost data=cas.train_mean_oofs outmodel=cas.gbt_ensemble;
    target target / level=nominal;
    input mean_factmac mean_gbt mean_logit mean_frst / level=interval;
    autotune tuningparameters=(ntrees samplingrate vars_to_try(init=4)
            learningrate(ub=0.3) lasso ridge) searchmethod=random
            samplesize=200 objective=ase kfold=5;
    ods output FitStatistics=Work._Gradboost_FitStats_
            VariableImportance=Work._Gradboost_VarImp_;
run;
```

The OUTMODEL option in the PROC statement saves the resulting trained model as a CAS table called gbt_ensemble. This table is used later for scoring the test data. The TARGET statement specifies the binary target variable, and the INPUT statement specifies the average OOF predictions that are obtained from Level-2 average models for gradient boosting, forest, logistic regression, and factorization machines.

The AUTOTUNE statement performs an automatic search for the optimal hyperparameter settings of the gradient boosting algorithm. It specifies a random search among 200 randomly selected hyperparameter settings of the gradient boosting algorithm. For assessing the resulting models, five-fold cross validation is used with the ASE metric that is specified by the following suboptions of the AUTOTUNE statement: OBJECTIVE=ASE KFOLD=5. The AUTOTUNE statement performs a search for the following parameters of the gradient boosting algorithm: number of iterations, sampling proportion, number of variables to try, learning rate, and LASSO and ridge regularization parameters. For other parameters, the procedure uses default values (the maximum depth of a tree is 5, the maximum number of observations for a leaf is 5, and the maximum number of branches for a node is 2), but these values can also be optionally tuned. To further control the parameter search process, you can specify upper bounds, lower bounds, and initial values for the hyperparameters. The preceding statements specify an upper bound for the learning rate parameter, LEARNINGRATE (UB=0.2), and an initial value for the number of variables to try, VARS_TO_TRY (INIT=4).

Figure 4 summarizes the autotuning options that are specified in the AUTOTUNE statement.

Tuner Information	
Model Type	Gradient Boosting Tree
Tuner Objective Function	Average Squared Error
Search Method	RANDOM
Maximum Evaluations	201
Sample Size	200
Maximum Tuning Time in Seconds	36000
Validation Type	Cross-Validation
Num Folds in Cross-Validation	5
Log Level	2
Seed	1669463436

Figure 4. Autotuning Information Table

Figure 5 shows the resulting best configuration hyperparameter values.

Best Configuration	
Evaluation	86
Number of Trees	56
Number of Variables to Try	3
Learning Rate	0.10990335
Sampling Rate	0.75938235
Lasso	3.25403452
Ridge	3.64367127
Average Squared Error	0.09

Figure 5. Autotuning Best Hyperparameter Settings for the Stacking Gradient Boosting Model

The "Tuner Summary" table in Figure 6 shows that the five-fold ASE for the best configuration of hyperparameter values is 0.09245.

Tuner Summary	
Initial Configuration Objective Value	0.09330
Best Configuration Objective Value	0.09245
Worst Configuration Objective Value	0.1448
Initial Configuration Evaluation Time in Seconds	10.4112
Best Configuration Evaluation Time in Seconds	9.2367
Number of Improved Configurations	5
Number of Evaluated Configurations	201
Total Tuning Time in Seconds	300.98
Parallel Tuning Speedup	10.1676

Figure 6. Autotuning Summary Table for the Stacking Gradient Boosting Model

Figure 6 also reports the total tuning time to be 5 minutes. This time is based on using 100 nodes in a SAS Viya distributed analytics platform. Note that five-fold cross validation is used as an assessment measure and models are assessed for 200 different hyperparameter settings, which requires fitting and scoring for 1,000 models. Each training set includes approximately 25,600 samples (4/5 of the full training set) and 4 features, and training and scoring for one model took around 0.35 seconds. This brief amount of time is made possible by taking full advantage of in-memory parallel computing not only for running each gradient boosting model but also for performing a random search for hyperparameter tuning.

The output also includes a table of the parameter settings and the corresponding five-fold ASEs for all 200 hyperparameter settings. Figure 7 shows the best 10 models that are found by the autotuning functionality. The AUTOTUNE statement in SAS Viya machine learning procedures has even more extensive capabilities that are not covered here; for more information and full capabilities, see Koch et al. (2017).

Tuner Results **Default and Best Configurations**							
Evaluation	Number of Trees	Number of Variables to Try	Learning Rate	Sampling Rate	Lasso	Ridge	Average Squared Error
0	100	4	0.100000	0.500000	0	0	0.0933
86	56	3	0.109903	0.759382	3.254035	3.643671	0.0924
78	84	3	0.078068	0.618316	7.852888	3.410856	0.0925
17	93	2	0.074230	0.545497	2.438973	1.077369	0.0925
149	76	3	0.149835	0.991542	6.293911	3.741891	0.0926
37	61	3	0.096917	0.574695	3.551582	2.478200	0.0926
108	76	4	0.066486	0.681446	8.874643	6.520876	0.0926
117	52	2	0.191996	0.959816	0.214059	5.811560	0.0926
40	54	3	0.109288	0.778913	9.021802	0.708567	0.0926
129	65	3	0.069800	0.851765	5.150564	0.671172	0.0926
126	50	3	0.104418	0.808189	9.780431	0.641345	0.0926

Figure 7. Autotuning Results for the Best 10 Models

Figure 8 plots the variable importance for the selected hyperparameter settings of the gradient boosting model. The two tree-based methods dominate.

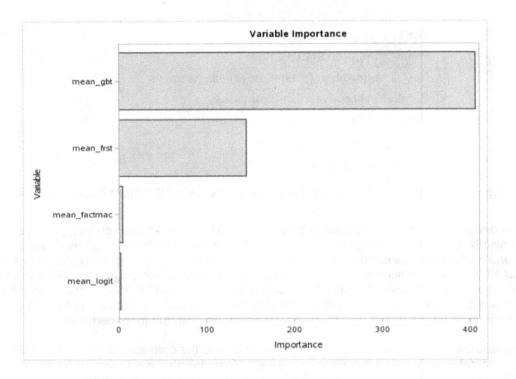

The following PROC GRADBOOST statements use the saved stacked ensemble model (cas.gbt_ensemble) to score the test set. The input data set (cas.test_mean_preds) includes Level-2 predictions for the test set.

```
proc gradboost data=cas.test_mean_preds inmodel=cas.gbt_ensemble;
    output out=cas.test_gbtscr copyvars=(id target);
run;
```

The following SAS code calculates the test ASE for the gradient boosting stacked ensemble model for the test data:

```
data cas.test_gbtscr;
    se=(p_target1-target)*(p_target1-target);
run;

proc cas;
    summary/ table={name='test_gbtscr', vars={'se'}};
run;
quit;
```

The **summary** action reports the ASE of the test data as 0.09298.

PROC GRADBOOST runs the **gbtreetrain** and **gbtreescore** CAS actions (in the Decision Tree action set) behind the scenes to train and score gradient boosting models. Appendix A provides a step-by-step CAS language (CASL) program that uses these actions to find the five-fold OOF predictions and cross validation ASE of the model for the hyperparameter values that are found here. Programming through CASL and CAS actions often requires more coding compared to using packaged machine learning procedures, which are essentially bundled functions of CAS actions. However, programming this way offers you more flexibility and control over the whole model building process. You can also call CAS actions through other languages such as Python and Lua.

HILL CLIMBING

The hill climbing technique (Caruana et al. 2004) is similar to forward stepwise selection. At each step of the selection, the model in the model library that maximizes the preferred performance metric joins the ensemble, and the ensemble is updated to be a simple weighted average of models. Hill climbing differs from regular stepwise selection in that rather than fitting a linear model at each step of the selection, it adds models to an ensemble by averaging predictions with the models already in the ensemble. As such, it is actually a form of nonnegative least squares, because the coefficients of each model are guaranteed to be nonnegative. Building an ensemble model this way can be very efficient computationally and has the significant advantage of being readily applicable to any performance metric of interest.

Caruana et al. (2004) use a hill climbing (single holdout validation) set at each step of the selection process to assess model performance. A separate validation set plays an important role in order to deal with overfitting, especially when you use the regular training predictions as input variables. However, instead of using a hill climbing validation set, this paper's analysis performs hill climbing on the library of OOF predictions. This approach deals with overfitting while maximally using the training data for the critical hill climbing step.

At each iteration of the hill climbing algorithm, every candidate model is evaluated to find the one that maximally improves the ensemble in a greedy fashion. Selection with replacement allows models to be added to the ensemble multiple times, permitting an already used model to be selected again rather than adding an unused model (which could possibly hurt the ensemble model's performance). Thus each model in the ensemble model can take different weights based on how many times it is selected.

For the Adult data, an ensemble model is built by using hill climbing for combining the four average Level-2 models. Figure 8 shows that the first model to enter the ensemble is the single best gradient boosted tree (gbt) model with a five-fold training cross validation ASE of 0.09235. Hill climbing keeps adding the same gradient boosting model until step 7. At step 7, the forest model joins the ensemble, which helps decrease both the training and testing errors nicely.

Obs	Step	Model	ASE_test	ASE_train		Obs	Step	Model	ASE_test	ASE_train
1	1	mean_gbt	0.092734	0.09235		10	10	mean_gbt	0.092678	0.09233
2	2	mean_gbt	0.092734	0.09235		11	11	mean_gbt	0.092679	0.09233
3	3	mean_gbt	0.092734	0.09235		12	12	mean_gbt	0.092680	0.09233
4	4	mean_gbt	0.092734	0.09235		13	13	mean_gbt	0.092682	0.09233
5	5	mean_gbt	0.092734	0.09235		14	14	mean_gbt	0.092684	0.09233
6	6	mean_gbt	0.092734	0.09235		15	15	mean_gbt	0.092685	0.09233
7	7	mean_frst	0.092684	0.09235		16	16	mean_gbt	0.092687	0.09233
8	8	mean_gbt	0.092679	0.09234		17	17	mean_gbt	0.092689	0.09233
9	9	mean_gbt	0.092678	0.09233		18	18	mean_gbt	0.092690	0.09233
10	10	mean_gbt	0.092678	0.09233		19	19	mean_gbt	0.092692	0.09233
						20	20	mean_gbt	0.092693	0.09233

Figure 8. First 20 Steps of Hill Climbing

Figure 9 shows graphically how the training and test errors change by the hill climbing steps. It shows that after step 9, the training error does not change much, but the test error increases slightly. The model at step 9 has a training ASE of 0.09268 and a testing ASE of 0.09233. If you choose this model at step9 as the final hill climbing model, the Level-2 average gradient boosting model takes a weight of 8, the Level-2 average forest model takes a weight of 1, and the other two models take 0 weights. In a typical hill climbing ensemble model, it is common to see powerful models being selected multiple times. In this case, the gbt model dominates but is complemented by a small contribution from forest model.

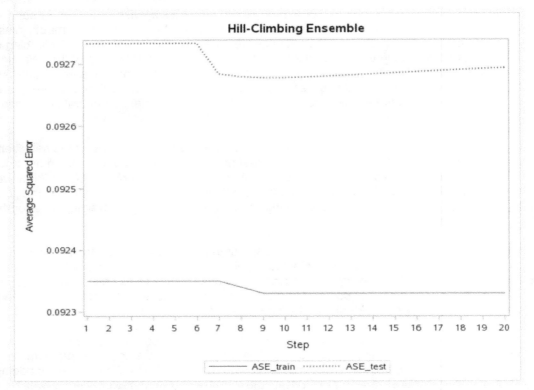

Figure 9. First 20 Steps of Hill Climbing with the Corresponding Training and Test ASEs

Because the hill climbing SAS program is lengthy, it is not provided here. See the GitHub repository for the full hill climbing program, which is written in the CAS language. The program is very flexible, and you can run it in the SAS Viya environment to build your own hill climbing ensemble model for your data.

When the same objective function is used, the nonnegative least squares approach is a generalization of hill climbing technique. For this example, Figure 10 shows that all three Level-3 linear modeling approaches (adaptive LASSO, nonnegative least squares, and hill climbing) produced very similar results and decreased the test ASE when compared to the single best model of Level-2 (shown in last row). On the other hand, the Level-3 stacked gradient boosting model did not provide a better model than the Level-2 average gradient boosting model.

Note that since the adaptive LASSO and the nonnegative least squares models weights are so close to each other, the training and test ASEs are almost the same when five decimal points are used. Note also that training ASEs are calculated when the Level-3 models are fit on the full training data.

Models	Training ASE	Test ASE
Level-3 adaptive LASSO	0.09269	0.09228
Level-3 nonnegative least squares	0.09269	0.09228
Level-3 gradient boosting	0.09130	0.09298
Level-3 hill climbing	0.09268	0.09233
Level-2 best model: average gradient boosting	**0.09236**	**0.09273**

Figure 10. Level-3 Stacked Models Training and Test ASEs Compared to the Single Best Level-2 Model

CONCLUSION

Stacked ensembling is an essential tool in any expert data scientist's toolbox. This paper shows how you can perform this valuable technique in the new SAS Viya framework by taking advantage of powerful underlying machine learning algorithms that are available through CAS procedures and actions.

REFERENCES

Breiman, L. 1995. "Stacked Regressions." *Machine Learning* 24:49–64.

Caruana, R., Niculescu-Mizil, A., Crew, G., and Ksikes, A. 2004. "Ensemble Selection from Libraries of Models." *Proceedings of the Twenty-First International Conference on Machine Learning*. New York: ACM.

Cawley, G. C., and Talbot, N. L. 2010. "On Over-fitting in Model Selection and Subsequent Selection Bias in Performance Evaluation." *Journal of Machine Learning Research* 11:2079–2107.

Dietterich, T. 2000. "Ensemble Methods in Machine Learning." *Lecture Notes in Computer Science* 1857:1–15.

Güneş, F. 2015. "Penalized Regression Methods for Linear Models in SAS/STAT." Cary, NC: SAS Institute Inc. Available at https://support.sas.com/rnd/app/stat/papers/2015/PenalizedRegression_LinearModels.pdf.

Hastie, T. J., Tibshirani, R. J., and Friedman, J. H. 2001. *The Elements of Statistical Learning: Data Mining, Inference, and Prediction.* New York: Springer-Verlag.

Koch, P., Wujek, B., Golovidov, O., and Gardner, S. 2017. "Automated Hyperparameter Tuning for Effective Machine Learning." In *Proceedings of the SAS Global Forum 2017 Conference.* Cary, NC: SAS Institute Inc. Available at http://support.sas.com/resources/papers/ proceedings17/SAS514-2017.pdf.

Lichman, M. 2013. UCI Machine Learning Repository. School of Information and Computer Sciences, University of California, Irvine. Available at http://archive.ics.uci.edu/ml.

Sill, J., Takacs, G., Mackey, L., and Lin, D. 2009. "Feature-Weighted Linear Stacking." CoRR abs/0911.0460.

Tibshirani, R. 1996. "Regression Shrinkage and Selection via the Lasso." *Journal of the Royal Statistical Society*, Series B 58:267–288.

Van der Laan, M. J., Polley, E. C., and Hubbard, A. E. 2007. "Super Learner." *U.C. Berkeley Division of Biostatistics Working Paper Series*, Working Paper 222.

Wexler, J., Haller, S., and Myneni, R. 2017. "An Overview of SAS Visual Data Mining and Machine Learning on SAS Viya." In *Proceedings of the SAS Global Forum 2017 Conference.* Cary, NC: SAS Institute Inc. Available at http://support.sas.com/resources/papers/ proceedings17/SAS1492-2017.pdf.

Wujek, B., Hall, P., and Güneş, F. 2016. "Best Practices in Machine Learning Applications." In *Proceedings of the SAS Global Forum 2016 Conference.* Cary, NC: SAS Institute Inc. Available at https://support.sas.com/resources/papers/proceedings16/SAS2360-2016.pdf.

Zou, H. 2006. "The Adaptive Lasso and Its Oracle Properties." *Journal of the American Statistical Association* 101:1418–1429.

ACKNOWLEDGMENTS

The authors are grateful to Wendy Czika and Padraic Neville of the Advanced Analytics Division of SAS for helpful comments and support. The authors also thank Anne Baxter for editorial assistance.

RECOMMENDED READING

A GitHub repository is available at https://github.com/sassoftware/sas-viya-machine-learning/stacking.The repository contains several different programs to help you reproduce results in this paper. The repository also contains supplemental material, including a detailed breakdown of some additional ensembling that is performed using Level-2 bootstrap samples.

Getting Started with SAS® Visual Data Mining and Machine Learning

SAS® Visual Data Mining and Machine Learning : Data Mining and Machine Learning Procedures

SAS® Visual Data Mining and Machine Learning : Statistical Procedures

SAS® Econometrics: Econometrical Procedures

SAS® Visual Data Mining and Machine Learning : Data Mining and Machine Learning Programming Guide

SAS® Cloud Analytic Services: CAS Procedure Programming Guide and Reference

CONTACT INFORMATION

Your comments and questions are valued and encouraged. Contact the authors:

Funda Güneş
SAS Institute Inc.
funda.gunes@sas.com

Russ Wolfinger
SAS Institute Inc.
Russ.Wolfinger@jmp.com

Pei-Yi Tan
SAS Institute Inc.
Pei-Yi.Tan@sas.com

APPENDIX A:

This appendix provides a step-by-step CAS language program that calculates and saves five-fold OOF predictions of the stacked ensemble model with the scalable gradient boosting algorithm for the set of hyperparameters that are shown in Figure 5. You can easily modify this program to obtain OOF predictions for your models that might use different machine learning training and scoring CAS actions.

```
/* Start a CAS session named mySession */
cas mySession;

/* Define a CAS engine libref for CAS in-memory data tables */
libname cas sasioca;

/* Create a SAS libref for the directory that has the data */
libname data "/folders/myfolders/";

/* Load OOF predictions into CAS using a DATA step */
data cas.train_oofs;
     set data.train_oofs;
     _fold_=int(ranuni(1)*5)+1;
run;

proc cas;
     /* Create an input variable list for modeling*/
     input_vars={{name='mean_gbt'},{name='mean_frst'},{name='mean_logit'},
               {name='mean_factmac'}};
     nFold=5;
```

```
    do i=1 to nFold;
        /* Generate no_fold_i and fold_i variables */
        no_fold_i = "_fold_ ne " || (String)i;
        fold_i    = "_fold_ eq " || (String)i;

        /* Generate a model name to store the ith trained model */
        mymodel = "gbt_" || (String)i;

        /* Generate a cas table name to store the scored data */
        scored_data = "gbtscore_" || (String)i;

        /* Train a gradient boosting model without fold i */
        decisiontree.gbtreetrain result=r1 /
            table={name='train_mean_oofs',  where=no_fold_i}
            inputs=input_vars
            target="target"
            maxbranch=2
            maxlevel=5
            leafsize=60
            ntree=56
            m=3
            binorder=1
            nbins=100
            seed=1234
            subsamplerate=0.75938
            learningRate=0.10990
            lasso=3.25403
            ridge=3.64367
            casout={name=mymodel, replace=1};
            print r1;

        /* Score for the left out fold i */
        decisionTree.gbtreescore result = r2/
            table={name='train_mean_oofs', where=fold_i}
            model={name=mymodel}
            casout={name=scored_data, replace=TRUE }
            copyVars={"id", "target"}
            encodeName=true;
    end;
quit;

/* Put together OOF predictions */
data cas.gbt_stack_oofs (keep= id target p_target se);
    set cas.gbtscore_1-cas.gbtscore_5;
    se=(p_target-target)*(p_target-target);
    run;
run;

/* The mean value for variable se is the 5-fold cross validation error */
proc cas;
    summary / table={name='gbt_stack_oofs', vars={'se'}};
run;
/* Quit PROC CAS */
quit;
```

www.ingramcontent.com/pod-product-compliance
Lightning Source LLC
Chambersburg PA
CBHW080533060326
40690CB00022B/5109

Check out these related books in the SAS® bookstore:

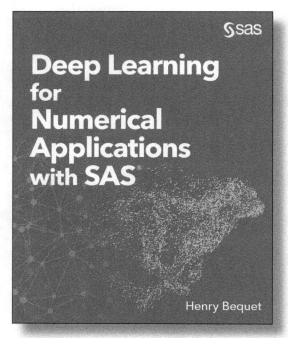

Deep Learning for Numerical Applications with SAS®

Henry Bequet

BIG DATA, DATA MINING, AND MACHINE LEARNING

Value Creation for Business Leaders and Practitioners

Jared Dean

WILEY

Decision Trees for Analytics Using SAS® Enterprise Miner™

Barry de Ville and Padraic Neville

For 20% off these e-books, visit **sas.com\books** and use the code WITHSAS20